A
SECRET
WELL KEPT

Acknowledgements

In writing this book I have had the generous help of Alison Moreira who did all the typing. To her go my most grateful thanks – also to my son John, to Sheila Davies and to my two granddaughters, Phillida Robertson and Bridget Kell – and in particular to my son James, to whom I owe the encouragement to write the tale of my husband's life in the Far East and of the task he undertook a few years later, on his return to England.

CRK
1959

A SECRET WELL KEPT

THE UNTOLD STORY OF SIR VERNON KELL
FOUNDER OF
MI5

CONSTANCE KELL

Foreword by Caroline Coverdale,
great-granddaughter of Sir Vernon and Lady Kell

Introduction by Stewart Binns

Notes by Chris Northcott

C
CONWAY
BLOOMSBURY
LONDON · OXFORD · NEW YORK · NEW DELHI · SYDNEY

Conway
An imprint of Bloomsbury Publishing Plc

50 Bedford Square
London
WC1B 3DP
UK

1385 Broadway
New York
NY 10018
USA

www.bloomsbury.com

CONWAY and the 'C' logo are trademarks of Bloomsbury Publishing Plc

First published 2017

ISBN: HB: 978-1-8448-6435-5
ePDF: 978-1-8448-6432-4
ePub: 978-1-8448-6434-8

2 4 6 8 10 9 7 5 3 1

Typeset in Baskerville by Deanta Global Publishing Services, Chennai, India
Printed and bound in Great Britain by CPI Group (UK) Ltd, Croydon CR0 4YY

To find out more about our authors and books visit www.bloomsbury.com. Here you
will find extracts, author interviews, details of forthcoming events and the option
to sign up for our newsletters.

Publisher's Note: The original manuscript has been lightly edited to aid understanding for a modern
audience and to correct misspellings of names and proper nouns.

CONTENTS

CONTENTS

By Dr Chris Northcott, author and lecturer in
Intelligence and Security Studies

FOREWORD

❖

Recently, I made a fascinating discovery. Hidden away with a number of beautiful old photo albums lay an enchanting manuscript. It was written by my great-grandmother, about her life with her husband, Sir Vernon Kell. As soon as I started reading it, I became engrossed in their world and thought how wonderful it would be to share their remarkable story with others. In fact, I soon discovered that this had also been Lady Kell's wish.

I love her style of writing, her courage and tenacity. Her devotion to her husband is so deep and pure. She talks so fondly of Sir Vernon throughout the book, and emphasises how much he achieved for our country during two world wars, giving him the credit he so rightly deserves.

One example of Lady Kell's courage is highlighted in a newspaper article from the *Evening Standard* of 3 April 1961. She was only 20 years old when she married Vernon and travelled to China for their honeymoon. 'We'd only been there two weeks when the Boxer Revolt broke. My husband was recalled to the Army and I was left in the settlement with all those guns trained on our house. It was rather alarming.'

Sadly, I never had the privilege of meeting my great-grandmother. However, I now feel I've had the chance to get to know her by reading her manuscript and letters and hearing so many wonderful stories from her children and grandchildren.

When Sir Vernon died, Lady Kell wrote an extremely touching letter to one of her sons. She explained: 'My life's work seems to have been taken from me for I lived largely for him. Now I am trying to love him more grandly by getting to understand that the body is only a "seeming", not the REAL of us and that there should be no separation if I can forget myself and think only of him. He must be needed elsewhere, all his wonderful qualities of leadership, courage, insight, sympathy and understanding of the qualities of all and everyone who came in touch with him, must make him the instrument ready to God's own hand, to fashion him for some loving work.'

Her granddaughters Caroline and Bridget, daughters of her youngest son, John, were incredibly close to their grandmother and seemed to have spent the most amount of time with her over the years. 'When I think about Granny,' Bridget recalls, 'although we remained close until her death, I remember especially the times I spent with her as a child: the many "treats" at Harrods, uniform buying and many other adventures. But most of all I remember her kindness and tolerance, her light-hearted way of dealing with us and our childish views and her efforts to turn my sister, Caroline, and me, in an ever-changing world into "young ladies". How she laughed at our expressions of horror and disgust as we tried her breakfast yoghurt – a definite novelty in those days. But I also realised, perhaps subconsciously, that she possessed a deep faith and although she never tried to force her beliefs onto us, they nonetheless influenced me for the good.'

'My first memories of Granny Con,' Caroline fondly adds, 'go back to 1946 when, just after the war, she used to meet me from the school train at Paddington every holidays, keep me happy for a couple of days and then send me on to my parents in Germany (complete with school trunk). Quite an undertaking! I remember her as tiny but indomitable, not particularly strict, but she did admonish me for sitting in an un-ladylike way with my legs apart! She had a special way of kissing with her eyelashes – a "butterfly" kiss. Her skin was very soft and she had a rather naughty chuckle.'

Virginia, John's third daughter, also reminisces about her times with her grandmother. 'My younger sister Charlotte and I were occasionally taken to London for the day, mainly to shop for school-uniform items. The highlight of the day would be lunch with Granny Con. As children, this always felt like a rather formal occasion, as Granny and her sister

Vera would appear for lunch wearing hats. Lunch itself would be cranked up from the kitchen below in a dumb waiter by the Irish cook, who lived in the basement with her parrot! Granny Con was, however, despite her rather formal appearance, a soft and kind person. She would chat easily with us and take an interest in what we were doing and what we enjoyed. On our first visit we told her politely how delicious the jelly was and we then got jelly for pudding on every future visit. Looking back on her life, she was obviously an amazing lady and a very strong support to my grandfather throughout their life together. She has left me with many special childhood memories.'

Phillida, daughter of Lady Kell's daughter Margaret, adored her grandmother. She remembers: 'Having come from Scotland, I loved staying in London with my wonderful grandmother who I looked up to and respected. She was such a fun person, who had a great sense of humour, and what a wit! She was always there for us. I often feel she is still around me.'

'What I do remember about Granny Con,' Jamie, Margaret's son, recalls, 'was that she was great at keeping the family together and in touch, as staying with her at 67 Evelyn Gardens was always fun, and a good meeting point for other members of the family. She helped me enormously when I was trying to sort myself out as a teenager. She was a good listener and always gave good and wise advice, usually offered over a delicious cup of tea. The drawing room was ideal for this as one could escape to the garden afterwards for some exercise, and later Mrs Carney, the cook, together with the parrot, were downstairs ready to dispense an Irish joke or two.'

My own mother, Suzan, daughter of Lady Kell's eldest son James, also had a very strong connection with her grandmother. 'My first encounter with Granny Con was when I was six and my mother and I went to stay with her at 67 Evelyn Gardens. Granny had a rather "no-nonsense" approach and I learned to admire and respect her as I grew older. She obviously saw it as her mission to turn all her granddaughters into young ladies. "Can't you strap them in dear?" I remember her pleading as we waited in Piccadilly to meet my father! I stayed with her a lot in my teens, and became more closely connected with her beliefs and ideas. Granny was a Christian Scientist (a view that I did not exactly share) but she introduced me to a Doctor of Metaphysics, and years later I became one myself. Granny had great strength, drive and determination. The fact that she was very small in stature did in no way diminish her strong personality. She loved music, the arts and a colourful garden, and I truly loved to spend time with her whenever the opportunity arose.'

Understandably, our family holds Lady Kell in high esteem, and have great respect and admiration for her and her husband. But it's also clear that it's not just the family who holds such strong views and are aware of Sir Vernon's great qualities. In the days following his death, letters flooded in.

Lady Kell wrote to her son, James, explaining: 'The letters I have already got are really marvellous and saying the same of him. His brilliant and able accomplishment of his great work and leadership of a unique kind, knitting everyone together under his direction with that understanding and sympathetic touch, unfailing help, patience and quick grasp of events. A quite unusual foresight. A gift of friendship that all from the lowest to the highest felt enthused by and felt the wish to give of their best for whatever work was set for them. Many letters say, a great man who has done great things for his country and who, by the nature of the things he achieved, could only be inadequately recognised. He made his country secure in the last war and made it possible for it to be so again in this, said another letter. I feel that the letters show that not only was he great in the achievement of his aim in his career but also in his personal life among men. For all have recognised the greatness, goodness and strength in his character in quite an unusual degree. It is seldom that both the public and personal achievement of that sort is reached in one person.'

Sir Vernon's photo sits proudly on our mantlepiece at home, a constant reminder of an extraordinary man. His decency, values, morals and kindness, patience and passion for making our world a safer place, are among the many qualities my great-grandfather possessed. I see now that his wife also possessed these attributes. Together they must have made quite a team.

A Secret Well Kept took Lady Kell nearly seven years to write. It is an inspiring tale of their life together, and gives us an insight into the private life of the man who founded MI5 and was its leader for over 30 years. I hope you also find it an inspiring read.

Caroline Coverdale
Great-granddaughter of Sir Vernon and Lady Kell

INTRODUCTION

❧

For as long as humankind has waged war, informers, infiltrators and spies have brought their skills to bear to influence the outcome of the conflict. Espionage is certainly an ancient occupation. Brave, foolhardy, greedy or idealistic, spies have forged a unique place in history and have often made the difference between victory and defeat. Sun Tzu, the Chinese philosopher and military strategist, wrote in *The Art of War*, 2,500 years ago: 'What enables an intelligent government and a wise military leadership to overcome others and achieve extraordinary accomplishments is foreknowledge.'

The Roman emperor Hadrian organised the Empire's *Frumentarii* – its wheat collectors – into an empire-wide intelligence-gathering organisation. He used them to spy on everyone in his huge domain, including his wife, family and friends.

Sir Francis Walsingham was one of Britain's most famous spies. An Elizabethan statesman and diplomat, Walsingham was a principal secretary to Queen Elizabeth I from 1573 until his death in 1590. Using all the techniques of the grand spymaster – double agents, secret codes and code-breaking, agents provocateurs and covert propaganda and disinformation – he was able to protect the Queen from those who would do her harm at home and challenge her from overseas. He was instrumental in bringing about the execution of Mary Queen of Scots, and in defeating the Spanish Armada.

The subject of this book, Vernon George Waldegrave Kell, stepped into the murky world of intrigue and deception in the early days of the 20th century. The son of an army officer, he was born in 1873 in

Great Yarmouth. His mother was the daughter of a Polish émigré, Count Konarski, a decorated Polish Army surgeon. Kell's destiny seemed to be a career in the army. He graduated from the Royal Military Academy, Sandhurst, and was commissioned into the South Staffordshire Regiment in October 1894. A man of many gifts, courteous and charming, perhaps his greatest asset was his ability as a linguist. He spoke French, German, Italian and Polish and, through his extensive travels in the later years of the 1890s, soon acquired Chinese and Russian.

While in China, he was involved in the Boxer Rebellion (1899–1900) and worked for army intelligence in Tientsin, as well as acting as a foreign correspondent for the *Daily Telegraph*. An officer of obvious talents, he was promoted to captain in 1901. In 1902, he returned to London and began working at the War Office analysing German intelligence. This was to be a watershed for Kell.

The British Army had continued to undertake military intelligence operations since Elizabethan times. By the 19th century, they were organised under the umbrella of the Directorate of Military Intelligence. Its focus was intelligence about the military strengths and capabilities of enemies – or potential enemies – particularly during military conflicts.

Following criticisms of intelligence gathering before and during the Boer War, Britain's military intelligence structures began to be overhauled and its manpower increased. In 1904, the service in which Kell now worked was re-organised under a Director of Military Operations, James Grierson – a former military attaché in Berlin and veteran of the Boxer Rebellion and Boer War. He commanded four sections: MO1 – Strategy; MO2 – Foreign Intelligence (with eight country sub-sections, A to H); MO3 – Administration and Special Duties; MO4 – Topographical.

This was the environment where Kell applied his various talents, learned the nuances of intelligence gathering and encountered the many eccentric characters who occupied the bizarre world of espionage.

Apart from army and naval intelligence, there was also another ingredient in the intelligence 'mix' at the turn of the 20th century. The Metropolitan Police Special Branch had been formed in 1883 to counter the threat of Fenian (Irish Republican Brotherhood) terrorism. The Superintendent of Special Branch from 1893 was a mercurial Irishman from County Kerry, William Melville. Melville made a name for himself chasing anarchists and subversives, and for his role protecting British and foreign royalty.

Melville resigned as Superintendent of Special Branch in 1903. Upon his departure, he was called the 'most celebrated detective of the day' by *The Times* and was made a Member of the Royal Victorian Order in recognition of his role in protecting the royal family over many years. Melville was presented with a gold watch and chain by Kaiser Wilhelm II, for protecting him during various visits to Britain.

However, in a secret move known only to a few, Melville did not retire to the country but joined MO3 at the War Office, where he was to play a key role in Vernon Kell's story. Operating out of a nondescript office in Westminster and under the alias of 'W Morgan, General Agent', for the next six years Melville prepared the ground for Vernon Kell's new role and organisation. He wined and dined Europe's leading spymasters such as Gustav Steinhauer, a man known as 'The Kaiser's Master Spy' who had been trained by the Pinkerton National Detective Agency in Chicago, and Pyotr Rachkovsky, the head of Okhrana, the Tsar of Russia's security service.

Melville would take Steinhauer to dinner at Simpson's Grand Cigar Divan in the Strand, where they would drink heavily and smoke the finest cigars. Whenever Rachkovsky came to London, he was accompanied by several of his officers and took a suite of rooms at the Savoy. These were the kind of men – friends and foes alike – who were to be the models for the myths and realities of the modern-day spy, and the men Vernon Kell would have to use all his guile to control.

By 1907, Melville was operating almost alone and on the outer fringes of the War Office, and his warnings about the growing threat from German espionage were largely ignored. However, circumstances began to change. Britain's power in the world and the security of its borders rested almost entirely on the overwhelming strength of the Royal Navy.

Through Britain's network of spies, it became clear that the Kaiser had dreams for a German empire to match those of France and Britain, and that he had grand designs for his German High Seas Fleet. It was increasingly apparent that he intended to re-equip his navy such that it would be a serious threat to the supremacy of the Royal Navy.

Author and journalist William Le Queux had published his anti-German invasion fantasy, *The Invasion of 1910*, in 1906. It sold over a million copies and was given even greater circulation when it was serialised by Lord Northcliffe's *Daily Mail*. Details of the German invasion route were given prominence and sounded alarm bells across the English shires. The *Mail* added 80,000 to its circulation. Le Queux became a celebrity, and began to style himself as a secret agent and spy-catcher, and surrounded himself with a few like-minded men in his own voluntary Secret Service Department.

By the autumn of 1907, several politicians had begun to respond to the growing unease. For the first time, it became clear to several influential figures that the particular 'intelligence' focus of the army and navy on military materiel and capabilities was not broad enough in an ever more sophisticated world of rapid travel by ship and train, and ever-advancing forms of communication by telegraph and telephone. Similarly, it was obvious that, with a small number of exceptions such as William Melville, the police did not have the skills or the intellect to cope with the dark arts of espionage.

In other words: spies were becoming more shadowy and operating in darker corners, and a new breed of counter-intelligence operatives had to be recruited to find and defeat them.

With Cabinet approval, Richard Haldane, Secretary of State for War in Asquith's Liberal Government, set up and chaired a sub-committee of the Committee of Imperial Defence in March 1909, to consider 'the nature and extent of foreign espionage that is at present taking place within the country and the danger to which it may expose us'.

Much of the evidence to the sub-committee was presented by Major James Edmonds, the head of a new section of the Directorate of Military

Operations, MO5 – responsible for Special Operations. Another remarkable figure, Edmonds was an experienced intelligence officer and regarded as the leading military intellectual of his generation. He was admitted into Sandhurst with the best marks the examiners could remember, passed out first in his year and first at Staff College. He was gazetted to the Royal Engineers, where his talents led to him being nicknamed *Archimedes*. A gifted linguist fluent in German, as a small boy living in France in 1870–1871 he had witnessed the advance of the German Army during the Franco-Prussian War. This had a profound effect on him, and he became preoccupied with the strengths and tactics of the German military machine.

By 1909, Edmonds was convinced that German espionage in Britain was a very real threat. In February he wrote: 'A German general landing a force in East Anglia would know more about the country than any British general, more about each town than its own British Mayor, and would have his information so methodically arranged that he could, in a few minutes, give you the answer to any question you asked him about any town, village or position in the area.'

Edmonds stressed to the sub-committee that neither army nor naval intelligence had the skills nor resources to counter German espionage, and that the police had been unable to detect a single case of recent German spying, despite his evidence that there had been five cases in 1907, 47 in 1908 and 24 in the first three months of 1909.

Haldane's sub-committee was convinced, and agreed unanimously that 'an extensive system of German espionage exists in this country' and recommended the establishment and funding of a 'Secret Service Bureau', to 'deal both with espionage in this country and with our own foreign agents abroad, and to serve as a screen between the Admiralty and the War Office on the one hand and those employed on secret service, or who have information they wish to sell to the British Government on the other.' The Bureau was to be so secret, its existence was known only to a few senior Whitehall mandarins and ministers – and so it remained for many decades.

So Britain's modern-day network of espionage and counter-espionage was born. The sub-committee recommended that 'two ex-naval and military officers should be appointed' (to the Bureau) 'having special qualifications'. The two men chosen were Army Captain Vernon Kell and Commander Mansfield Cumming of the Royal Navy.

The 50-year-old Cumming was perhaps a surprising choice. Born into a middle-class family, the son of a Nottingham engineer, he joined the Royal Navy at the age of 12. He was posted to HMS *Bellerophon* and served on operations against Malay pirates for seven years. In 1883 he was posted to Egypt, but acute seasickness cut short his career at sea and he was placed on the retired list as 'unfit for service'.

When he was appointed to the Secret Service Bureau (SSB), Cumming was working on boom defences in Bursledon on the River Hamble. Jovial and extrovert, and prone to fanciful stories and exaggeration, to some he seemed to possess few of the talents necessary for the world of espionage.

Vernon Kell, 14 years Cumming's junior, was, on the other hand, an ideal fit. Recommended by Edmonds for the role, he was widely travelled, sophisticated and charming, and had a remarkable grasp of languages. Moreover, he had been working in military intelligence since 1902.

Such was the secrecy surrounding the SSB, both Cumming and Kell had to be removed from the active list and thus put their professional futures at great risk. As Vernon's wife Constance later wrote: 'There was the risk that should he fail to carry it through, it would leave him with his career wrecked and bring about the dismal prospect of having to provide for his family with no adequate means of doing it.' But Constance knew her husband well. She added: 'He was young and an optimist – why should he fail?'

There were soon tensions between Kell and Cumming. Their respective roles had not been clearly defined, and Cumming in particular felt he was being marginalised and seen as Kell's deputy. However, a compromise was reached, which would have a lasting impact on Britain's intelligence infrastructure.

In October 1909, Kell and Cumming agreed a division of duties. Kell was given the home intelligence work, both naval and military (MI5). Cumming was assigned the foreign work, both naval and military (SIS, later known as MI6). It is a division that persists to this day.

The split worked well. Kell spent the early months 'going through the previous history of counter-espionage as shown in the War Office files, and in getting acquainted with the various aspects of the work.'

Kell had to run his operation on a shoestring budget, with William Melville as his assistant. In March 1910, he was given permission to engage a clerk. The Bureau's first officer recruit joined in January 1911. By August 1914, the Bureau had grown to six officers, Melville and two other detectives, six clerks, and a caretaker. With scant resources, the key to Kell's strategy was to gain the support of police chief constables, and for this he needed the assistance of the Home Secretary, who for most of 1910–1911 was Winston Churchill. Churchill had a greater appreciation of intelligence than any other British politician of his generation. In the summer of 1910, with helpful letters of introduction from Churchill and the Secretary of State for Scotland, Kell contacted 35 English chief constables and seven Scottish chief constables, 'who all expressed themselves most willing to assist me in every way.'

Kell's charisma and powers of persuasion began to pay off. The charming soldier who had been dubbed 'the man with the golden tongue' began to make his mark. Using his contacts from all over the world, he laid the foundations of Britain's modern counter-espionage operations. The Aliens Sub-Committee of the Committee of Imperial Defence, founded in March 1910, was chaired by Churchill, who approved Kell's preparation of a secret register of aliens from likely enemy powers, primarily Germany, based upon information provided by local police forces. Chief constables were asked to report: 'Any specific acts of espionage on the part of the reported on; or other circumstances of an unusual nature.'

For a while, the quality of intelligence did not improve, but Kell reached two main conclusions from the first six months of the existence of the Bureau (Kell's name for his operation):

(a) The Bureau has justified its institution;

(b) The experience gained has proved that it is essential to the effective working of the Counter-espionage Section of the Bureau that all information coming within its province should be sent to and exclusively dealt with by the Bureau.

Despite the positive tone, Kell, ever the optimist, was fighting significant odds. He was under-resourced, under-manned and trying to break new ground: not an enviable position. Although information did begin to flow from police reports around the country, it was often based on hearsay, was prone to exaggeration and was sometimes erroneous.

However, Kell persevered. Then, Churchill made a decision that greatly enhanced the Bureau's work. Against Post Office advice, he extended the Home Office Warrant system, which allowed warrants to be issued to permit the opening and examination of the correspondence of suspects.

Gradually, more men and resources were made available to the Bureau. Then Kell benefitted from an extraordinary piece of serendipity. In January 1911, he appointed Captain Stanley Clarke, an army officer who had served in India for 11 years, as his assistant. In August of that year, Clarke happened to share a railway carriage with a Francis Holstein, who ran the Peacock Hotel in Newhaven Harbour on the Firth of Forth. Clarke overheard Holstein talking with a friend about an unsolicited letter he had received from an 'F Reimers' in Potsdam, asking for information about British public opinion and preparations for a future war. Delving further into this, it was discovered that F Reimers was in fact Gustav Steinhauer, Germany's spymaster!

This astonishing stroke of luck coupled with the Home Office Warrants meant that Kell could compile a detailed cross-referenced index of intercepted letters between German intelligence and its agents in Britain. Intelligence gathering improved, and arrests followed.

As Constance had observed, Vernon was not going to fail. His operation was going to be a resounding success. Perhaps the most important German spy to be uncovered before the outbreak of the Great War was Frederick Adolphus Schroeder, who took the alias Gould. He had an English mother and German father, and in 1908 became the licensee of a pub in Chatham. He travelled to Germany with his wife on several occasions, taking with him classified information. Gould reported directly to Gustav Steinhauer, the Kaiser's spymaster, and became a family friend. Kell had had his letters to Steinhauer intercepted and was diligently monitoring his correspondence. Kell decided to act. Gould's wife was arrested at Charing Cross Station in February 1914. She was carrying a gunnery drill booklet and charts of Spithead and Bergen. Gould was arrested on the same day, and later sentenced to six years' hard labour.

Shrewdly, Kell preferred to monitor most of his suspects rather than arrest them. In that way, he could record their activities and build up an ever more sophisticated map of the German network. He was also wary of the implications of the British legal system, saying, 'it was considered contrary to the interests of the State to bring some men to trial, which would have entailed a disclosure of the identity of our informants and other confidential matters.'

Kell developed a precise system for the storage of information, which may seem mundane by the standards of modern-day computer-based methods, but at the time was a fundamental breakthrough. He introduced a Roneo Card indexing system to record the vital details of all suspects or potential suspects. Yellow or red wafer seals were added to the cards of those under the greatest suspicion. Yellow meant 'possible suspect', red meant 'Special War List' – high-risk individuals subject to regular monitoring. In addition to the red seal, a single X on a card meant the individual had to be searched on the outbreak of war, while a double X meant the suspect had to be arrested as soon as war was declared. It was simple, but crucial to the success of the early days of MI5.

In under five years, Kell transformed British counter-espionage. Given the Bureau's limited resources, its achievements are even more impressive. Recent archival research in Germany shows that the Bureau did not manage to detect all of the German agents operating in Britain at the outbreak of the First World War. The Bureau did, however, succeed in rounding up all of the German spies that mattered. There is no evidence that any useful intelligence from Britain reached Germany in the crucial first few weeks of the war. As Eric Holt-Wilson (Kell's deputy from 1912) later observed: 'A German Order came into our hands early in the war which disclosed the fact that as late as 21 August [ie 17 days after war was declared], the German Military Commanders were still ignorant of the despatch and movements of our Main Expeditionary Force, although this had been more or less common knowledge to thousands in this country.'

With the outbreak of war, new legislation provided the authorities with unprecedented powers to handle aliens and suspected spies. The Aliens Restriction Act, prepared by the Home Office in concert with Kell and Holt-Wilson in readiness for war, was passed by Parliament on 5 August 1914. It gave the authorities virtually unlimited powers 'to impose restrictions on aliens and make such provisions as appear necessary or expedient for carrying such restrictions into effect.' The Defence of the Realm Act (DORA), also prepared with the assistance of Kell and Holt-Wilson, became law on 8 August 1914. It provided the government with powers close to martial law. The game had changed.

Twenty-two German agents were arrested at the outbreak of war, and another seven over the next year. Eleven men were executed, including Irish Nationalist, Sir Roger Casement, who was found guilty of treason in 1916. Kell was made Companion of the Order of the Bath (CB) in 1917 and knighted as Knight Commander of the Order of the British Empire in 1919.

By the 1920s, the focus of Kell's counter-espionage work had also changed. The Bolshevik Revolution in Russia had created new threats to Britain's security, and 'subversives' of many shades came under scrutiny.

In October 1931, the lead role in countering Communist subversion moved from the Special Branch to MI5. MI5 became known as the Security Service. MI5 also acquired Scotland Yard's leading experts on subversion. The Security Service ceased being a section of the War Office. It acquired an enhanced, but ill-defined, status as an inter-departmental intelligence service working for the Home, Foreign, Dominion and Colonial Offices, service departments, the Committee of Imperial Defence, the Attorney General, the Director of Public Prosecutions and chief police officers in the UK and throughout the British Empire. A lot of lords and masters to please!

MI5's staff began to increase slightly from 1934 onwards. The budget for 1935–1936 was £25,000. This increased to £50,000 in 1938, and rose to £93,000 for 1939–1940. By January 1938, MI5 employed 26 officers and 80 Registry staff. By July 1939, this had grown to 36 officers and 133 Registry staff. MI5 broadened its international horizons during the 1930s. It began posting permanent liaison officers to some of Britain's overseas territories, to counter the threat from the Comintern and Rome–Berlin Axis operations. In 1937, MI5 posted its first permanent defence security officer (DSO) abroad at Cairo. DSOs were also posted to Palestine and Gibraltar in 1938. By the outbreak of the Second World War, there were also DSOs in Aden, Singapore and Hong Kong.

In 1932, the British Union of Fascists (BUF) was founded by Sir Oswald Mosley. MI5 began to target the BUF from 1934 onwards. At that time, the BUF had 35,000–40,000 members. Most of them just paid their subscriptions and purchased BUF publications, but active members numbered 10,000. Despite evidence of foreign funding for the BUF, the Home Secretary, Sir John Gilmour, refused MI5's application for surveillance of Mosley, believing that he remained an ardent patriot and no threat to Britain's national security.

However, in July 1937, the Committee of Imperial Defence approved a draft Bill, prepared by Kell and Holt-Wilson, allowing 'the detention of persons whose detention appears to the Secretary of State to be expedient in the interests of public security or the defence of the Realm.'

Thus, British citizens would no longer be exempt from internment, as they had been during the First World War. This laid the groundwork for the eventual internment of Mosley and many of his supporters in 1940.

By this time, Germany had replaced the USSR as the main target for British intelligence. In March 1936, Hitler had ordered troops into the Rhineland, in breach of the Treaty of Versailles. Britain took no military action.

However, Kell had begun to sense the danger of another world war. In June 1936, he sent the Committee of Imperial Defence a 'memorandum on the possibilities of sabotage by the organisations set up in British countries by the totalitarian governments of Germany and Italy.' It was probably the first memorandum circulated in Whitehall warning that negotiating with Hitler was not likely to achieve anything, and that Hitler's vast territorial ambitions laid out in *Mein Kampf* should be seen as a guide to his future conduct. Appeasement would not work. The only way to deal with Hitler was to stand firm.

In light of the Munich Crisis, in November 1938, Kell submitted a report to the Foreign Secretary, Lord Halifax, stating that in view of intelligence from reliable sources, he felt that: 'There is nothing surprising and nothing which could not have been foreseen in the events of this summer in connection with Czechoslovakia. These events are a logical consequence of Hitler's Nazi Weltanschauung and of his foreign policy and his views in regard to racial questions and the position of Germany in Europe.'

Kell aimed to stiffen the government's resolve by showing that Appeasement had encouraged, not reduced, Hitler's aggressive intentions. Kell concluded that Hitler was only in the early stages of a massive programme of territorial expansion. Eventually, in March 1939, Chamberlain finally told his Cabinet that: 'No reliance could be placed on any of the assurances given by the Nazi leaders'. This was a conclusion that Kell and MI5 had reached nearly three years earlier.

In December 1938, Kell, who was then 65 years old, had written to Sir Alexander Cadogan, Permanent Under-Secretary at the Foreign

Office, to ask 'in the interests of the Security Service, that something definite should be ordained with regard to my future ... I would suggest, if my work has been approved of, that my services should be retained on a yearly basis, provided that I am compos mentis and do not feel the burden too heavy.'

Whitehall had not given serious thought to the future management of the Security Service. Cadogan advised Sir Warren Fisher, head of the civil service, that Kell seemed 'active enough to carry on his present work efficiently, though one cannot of course tell how long that will continue to be the case. I should be quite content to see him continue for as long as he can.' Fisher saw Kell in January 1939, and agreed that he should continue on a yearly basis. He was promoted to Major-General later in the year, but he was 66 years old and his health was in decline.

Just before war was declared, MI5 had 36 officers (not including security control personnel at ports). This rose to 102 in January 1940. By January 1941, this stood at 230. In July 1939, MI5 had 133 secretarial and Registry staff. This increased to 334 in January 1940. It further increased to 617 in January 1941. Even with this increase in numbers, it was overwhelmed by the demands made on it by the commencement of a huge global conflict. It was also tasked with finding out if there was a fifth column of Nazi sympathisers in Britain and, if so, eliminating it.

By July 1940, 753 BUF members had been interned. There was also mass internment of enemy aliens. Between May and July 1940, approximately 22,000 Germans/Austrians and approximately 4,000 Italians were interned. By the fall of France in May 1940, MI5 was in a chaotic state. It just could not cope with the workload the politicians, especially the new Prime Minister, Winston Churchill, demanded of it. Kell was in his sixties and had already asked to continue on a year-by-year basis. However, the inexorable march of time and the extraordinary pressures of the grave military situation demanded that new blood be found. So, with typical forcefulness, Churchill insisted that Kell be 'retired'. Kell stepped down on 10 June 1940, as did his deputy, Eric Holt-Wilson.

A long and distinguished career in the service of his country was over. He was one of history's great spymasters and the longest-serving head of any British Government department in the 20th century.

Major-General Sir Vernon Kell died at his cottage, Stonepits, in Emberton, Buckinghamshire on 27 March 1942. He was 68 years old.

Stewart Binns
Author and filmmaker

1

MOSCOW

✤

I
t was in August 1909 that an opportunity arose for Vernon Kell to do something vitally necessary for the safety of his country. There was the risk that should he fail to carry it through it would leave him with his career wrecked and bring about the dismal prospect of having to provide for his family with no adequate means of doing it. But he was young and an optimist – why should he fail? I was sure he would succeed, so he decided to accept the suggestion of the Committee of Imperial Defence that he should start a scheme of special defence to counter espionage.[1] He was a fine linguist, that would be an asset; he had travelled a good deal and, best of all, he had vision.

He started off with high hopes, hardly knowing how to begin to lay the foundations of the organisation that eventually proved so successful. Even the enemies against whom the schemes were directed bore rather rueful testimony to their efficacy. In fact, they voiced grudging admiration of the way their network of spies was broken up and they found it necessary to alter their methods frequently, only to have them quickly checkmated.

Little did Vernon realise in those early days when he started with just one clerk that he was creating an organisation which would require the assistance of hundreds of people to operate, the number growing ever larger as the war years approached. He found that his experiences in China, and especially those relating to his work in connection with that of the temporary Russian Railway Administration during the Boxer

Rebellion, had given him an insight into the way the military minds of various foreign nationalities approached questions that required much vision to deal with and do so without friction.

Vernon liked to describe himself as a 'Yarmouth Bloater',[2] for it was at Yarmouth, where his mother[3] was spending a few days at the seaside, that he was born on November 21st 1873. He grew up with a cosmopolitan outlook, for his mother, a most attractive woman, was only half-English, her father, Count Konarski,[4] having married an English girl. The Count left Poland when many of the nobility and landed gentry had been pushed out during the unrestful days of the last century, and he had settled down to a rather uneventful country life in England.

Perhaps it was this touch of foreign blood in Vernon that accounted for the fact he was an excellent linguist, for he could, as a young man, speak six languages. He was educated privately, and it was at first intended that he should enter the Diplomatic Service, his name being placed on the personal list of Lord Salisbury, the prime minister.[5] This idea of a diplomatic career arose quite by chance from an incident that brought his name forward. As part of his studies, he was told to translate into four languages the address which Colonel Kenyon Slaney, then MP for Shropshire, had moved in the House of Commons in reply to the Queen's speech.[6] The Colonel was a great friend of the family, and the translations were sent to him more in joke than in earnest, but he was so struck with them that he showed them to Lord Salisbury, who promptly gave Vernon a nomination for the Diplomatic Service.

Vernon's father, Major Waldegrave Kell,[7] had started his army career in the Connaught Rangers,[8] then stationed in Ireland, and on the outbreak of the Zulu War[9] he went with his regiment to South Africa. Here, during the campaign against the Zulus, he very successfully carried out a most unusual task for an infantry officer. He was placed in command of a battery of artillery that had been left completely denuded of officers owing to wounds and sickness. He carried out this task so efficiently that it earned him a mention in dispatches, and he was given accelerated promotion and a job on the staff. One of his duties as a staff officer was to make arrangements for bringing back the body of the Prince Imperial to England for his funeral.[10] This prince, so beloved of his mother the Empress Eugenie, and in fact loved by all who knew him and served with him, had been ambushed and killed by the Zulus, a tragedy felt most deeply, especially by Queen Victoria, who knew what his death would mean to his mother.[11]

On his return from carrying out this duty, Waldegrave Kell was promoted to captain in the South Staffordshire Regiment and was made adjutant to the 4th Militia Battalion stationed at Lichfield.[12] He and his family went to live there, but his wife disliked his many moves to different stations while he was in the army and persuaded him to retire shortly after he had been promoted to major. They went to live in Shropshire at Ruckley Grange, a lovely house on a small estate where there was a certain amount of shooting, three small lakes and quite a good trout stream. Vernon soon became a good fisherman, and fishing remained always his favourite sport.

It was sometime after this that the question of a career for Vernon had to be decided. His father had suddenly and very unexpectedly decided to alter his plans for his entering the Diplomatic Service and now turned to the possibility of sending him into the army. Vernon was now just eighteen and could therefore only have one chance of passing the entrance examination before he reached the age limit. He was sent to a crammer, and succeeded in passing both his preliminary exam and his final within three months of each other.

In 1892 he went to Sandhurst and spent two very happy years there.[13] During his second year, a cadet arrived who was to become one of the most famous of men, namely Winston Churchill, who came with the reputation for being able to get away with most things, having been quite irrepressible at both his private and public schools.[14] But at Sandhurst he was determined to get through well. His imperturbable character, so individualistic and purposeful, got him into some difficulties and he had to undergo some pretty drastic ragging, but this completely failed in its object, for nothing could get him down and he passed out with nothing particularly arresting to relate while he was at Sandhurst. In later years Vernon was to see much more of him.

Vernon thoroughly enjoyed his time at Sandhurst, especially as he had been entirely free from asthma, which was the one great difficulty he had to contend with. From the time he was eight years old and in consequence of one of the usual infectious diseases of childhood, he was left with asthma, at first very severe, but later controllable except in certain localities. He was strong physically, but his affliction was always the thing he dreaded and had to fight against.

His father was now living in London and had married again, as his first wife had left him. Their house in Clarges Street was a delightful centre, for his American wife was a very charming hostess and they had a large circle of friends. Vernon liked his stepmother[15] greatly and spent many happy days there, but mostly he went abroad when he got leave and stayed with his French relations, who lived in the south of France and in Paris. His mother's two sisters, Countess Marie Konarska and Countess Emma Macswiney, lived in a lovely house at St Germain en Laye. They were known as 'the English ladies', though their very foreign accent seemed to belie that title considerably. Countess Emma had married a rich banker and was a wonderful horsewoman, with her own *haute école* on the premises. She was rather a haughty woman, very artistic, and had a great collection of antiques, so that her home resembled a museum. She chose to live like this, surrounded by glass cases, cabinets, statues of all sorts and no comfort anywhere, which was hard on poor Countess Marie, who loved her creature comforts. Vernon had many French cousins also and much enjoyed staying with them.

On completing his time at Sandhurst, Vernon joined his father's regiment, the 1st Battalion South Staffords, at Lichfield in October 1894. He went through the usual subaltern's courses, but he was determined to strike out on his own and make use of his languages. He therefore applied to go to Russia to get the Russian interpretership, which meant that he had to take a preliminary exam in London to qualify for it. While waiting for this he passed the French and German interpretership exams with ease. Having received permission to work for the Russian preliminary exam, he passed it successfully and could now go to Moscow to learn the language fluently.

In 1898 he got the necessary leave and went to live with a family called Von Kotzk in Moscow, where he could get the tuition he required. Madame Von Kotzk and her family were interesting, artistic, most amusing and lively. Madame took in boarders, British officers who were studying for the Russian interpretership, and she was a most excellent teacher. One of her pupils was a certain Captain Lindsay who had brought his wife and daughter with him. The little girl was a great favourite with them all and a very constant companion of Vernon's. What was their consternation when she suddenly developed scarlet fever, which in due course she handed on to Vernon. The question as to what to do with him was a puzzle, for there seemed nowhere else to send him but to the fever hospital in Moscow, where the accommodation was very primitive because the hospital at that time only catered for the very poor who could not afford to pay anything.

Vernon was driven to this hospital in a state of high fever in a one-horse tumbledown vehicle with all the windows broken. The cold was intense but he was feeling too ill to care much about that. On arrival his interest was certainly stimulated when he found himself bundled into a room where a woman managed to make him understand that he must have a bath before he could be allowed to get into bed. She prepared to attack him in the bath with a coarse wisp of straw to rub him down with, and a sort of circular piece of metal to scrape him with should he prove as dirty as most of the patients. On his protesting very vehemently she at last realised that her ministrations were not so very necessary, and she let him off. He was taken to a small private ward where fresh difficulties presented themselves. The mattress on the bed was of the coarsest straw, and as he lay on it with his skin so red and inflamed, the straws all stuck into his back and drove him frantic, his pillow no better. He knew enough Russian to beg the matron to allow him to buy a special mattress and pillow, and when she realised that he would pay she sent for them. At last he could get some ease, which was something to be thankful for, considering that he had bad attacks of asthma to add to all he was going through.

The matron and the nurses were very kind to him and took great interest in this young Englishman whose charm of manner and smiling resignation to the many discomforts he had to suffer attracted their sympathy and help. They found out that he was in Moscow to learn Russian and lost no opportunity to help him and to read to him; the matron, in particular, gave him as much of her time as she could spare and he learnt a great deal from her. The five weeks spent in hospital gave him quite an unlooked-for chance of becoming fluent in the language, and also it gave him an insight into the lives of the patients, who were very poor. He made great friends with them as soon as he was well enough to go into the public wards, and found them such simple, kindly people with the most trusting and childlike outlook on life, their ignorance quite astounding but their cheeriness most infectious. Vernon always spoke of his time in that hospital with great appreciation, for all the people he came in touch with had been so good to him and had made his convalescence very pleasant. He went back to the Von Kotzk family to continue his work and thoroughly enjoyed his time with them. They were such bright, intellectual people, always ready to make the best of difficulties, and they were many which came their way, for they had very little money and had a hard struggle to make two ends meet. Madame Von Kotzk herself, who did most of the teaching, introduced so much of interest into the lessons that it made it easier to learn what is, to most people, a very difficult language.

The winter passed quickly, a winter which gave Vernon an insight into all the brightness and light-heartedness of life in the Moscow of those days. The sunshine, the snow, the sleighs and their lovely teams of horses with jingling harness driven by fat drivers sitting perched up high and muffled to the ears; the expeditions to the hills for skiing, for skating; the dancing – all the gay Russian life made its appeal and Vernon felt the time slip away all too quickly. But his leave was up and he had to return to London to take the exam. This he passed very satisfactorily and then he rejoined his regiment, which was stationed at Spike Island in Cork Harbour.

They were good days in the South of Ireland, when there was so much prosperity in the towns owing to our troops stationed there, and HM ships. Trade flourished, money flowed freely, and there was a sense of security before the 'agitators' got busy among the people. The residents, both in town and country, lived in what seemed then a carefree atmosphere, in comparison to the strained uncertainties that were to follow when the unrest that led to what the Irish described as 'Our War' had settled upon them.

It was here that I first met Vernon. My father, James William Scott,[16] was a man well-known and much-beloved in that part of Ireland. Our family was a very musical one, which appealed to Vernon, for he could play the piano well and since his visit to Moscow had brought back some lovely Russian folk songs, which we thoroughly appreciated, for we sang well and this music was delightful. Vernon made many friends and enjoyed the genial gaiety of the people he met. He had plenty of sport of all sorts, and the friendly gaiety of everyone was so infectious that he enjoyed every moment of the amusing, careless life that all were sharing.

2

JOURNEY THROUGH
CANADA

❖

After a short spell of regimental life Vernon became restless and longed to go abroad again, and determined to ask once more for language leave, this time to go to China and try for the Chinese interpretership. His application succeeded and he started to make his plans to go off to Shanghai, when quite suddenly there came the fateful Jameson Raid[1] in South Africa, which so quickly led to the South African War.[2] Vernon naturally wanted to give up all thoughts of China and go with his regiment to the Cape, and his dismay was great when he was told he must stick to his original intention. He hurried over to London to see if a personal appeal to Major General Sir John Ardagh,[3] then Director of Military Intelligence, would succeed so that he could go to South Africa with his regiment. Sir John was very sympathetic, but also very emphatic; he could not alter his decision, and Vernon must leave for China as arranged. He cheered him up slightly by telling him that it would not surprise him if some active service might not be in store for him in the Far East.

Vernon went back to Spike Island bitterly disappointed, and very dejectedly continued his preparation for his journey to China. This was in the spring of 1900. His friendship for the Scott family had grown into a much closer bond. He wondered if I would perhaps consider going to China with him. We would have to get married straight away.

He came to me and asked what I thought about it. It was just wonderful, I gladly consented, for after all it would be a case of being only two years away, and why not go with him? Vernon had been seconded from his regiment for these two years to enable him to get the Chinese interpretership, but my mother was very alarmed at the prospect, though my father backed me up when we decided to marry early in April and go off. After a short honeymoon we spent a few days in Dublin, which was then crowded and beflagged, to greet Queen Victoria who was paying her last visit to Ireland, and we were there to take part in the great welcome she was given. We saw her several times as she drove through the streets; she looked pleased and happy, she had hardly expected the reception to be so spontaneous and the welcome from the crowds everywhere was most enthusiastic. We could only stay the inside of a week and left Dublin, going home to pick up our luggage and say goodbye.

On April 12th we went off in a tender to meet the liner that was to take us to New York. My mother looked very white and strained as she said goodbye, my father tried to be as gay as possible, and as we left the tender and waved to them from the deck of the liner we felt we had indeed taken a big step and wondered what lay in front of us. Our ship was due in New York on April 18th, and we planned to go by easy stages and eventually fetch up at Vancouver. The ship, the *Teutonic*, in those days one of the fastest ships of the White Star Line, was a good sea boat and she had need to be, for we encountered a very heavy storm in the Atlantic causing the ship to be a whole day late in arriving in New York. We reached the mouth of the Hudson River in dense fog and watched with intense interest the ship slowly and cautiously threading her way through much shipping. It seemed almost incredible that we did not collide with some of the ships that we barely scraped past. Just as we were nearing the Statue of Liberty the fog lifted, and the sight of the Statue of Liberty glittering in the sunshine, the shipping densely packed in the river, the marvellous silhouette of the tall, crowded buildings along the waterfront, was so beautiful that it made an unforgettable impression. Then came the bustle of docking, a perfect swarm of little tugs pushed and pulled the big liner and got her into place to enter the very narrow dock where she was to land her passengers. Soon gangways were moving on board, and everyone had to make ready for customs examinations.

We thought we had got through quite successfully when suddenly one of the officials caught sight of Vernon's sporting gun in its leather case. Now what would happen? For Vernon had forgotten to declare it. Well, after endless questions and a long hold-up, it was arranged that on payment of a very considerable sum of money and agreeing to the customs demand that a wooden packing case be made for it, it was to travel in bond by train to Vancouver and await our arrival there. We were then at last permitted to leave and find our hotel. I might say that when we did arrive at Vancouver and reclaimed the gun, it was still in its leather case unprotected by any wooden case for which we had paid so heavily! We were never quite so trusting again when confronted with customs requirements.

Friends of ours on board the liner had recommended us to go to a small hotel near the fashionable Waldorf Astoria. They said we could share in the fun at the big hotel, but pay less for our board and lodging in the small one. It was uncomfortable and rather antediluvian but served our purpose all right. We went out for a walk to take stock of our surroundings and were of course staggered at the height of the buildings, and that was in 1900! What would our consternation have been had we seen the buildings that are there now, for to us seventeen storeys was immensely high. The speed of the traffic in the streets surprised us, I rather hated that, and particularly having to rush in and out of a cable car or tram, run on a central road cable, which never came to a complete standstill. Crossing the streets seemed distinctly a voyage of adventure, for the traffic went at such pace that I breathed a sigh of relief when I got to the 'sidewalk' and could walk my own pace as slowly as I liked.

Friends of ours called Thomas (Mrs Thomas was a sister of Vernon's step-mother and a very charming woman) came to visit us in our hotel and took us on a sightseeing trip. First to Chinatown at night, where in a Chinese restaurant we sampled 'chop suey' which we were not especially pleased with, and watched a Chinaman with much fascination, eating macaroni from a bowl, never a gap in filling his mouth with the long strings which his chopsticks so deftly directed into it. Rice too, picked out grain by grain, in a never-ending stream until another bowl was emptied. After admiring the rather strange sights in this curious part of New York we returned to our hotel by elevated railway and streetcar.

The Thomases invited us to go and stay with them in Troy, which we were very delighted to do and get a glimpse of American family life, and we spent a few very happy days with them. They lived in a nice house with a flower and vegetable garden quite open to the road, anyone could walk in, but no one seemed to trespass and there seemed no need for hedges or railings. Everything was simple and labour-saving in the house; their Irish maid lived in a kitchen just like a sitting-room. She was a nice girl and felt as strange as I did in her new surroundings, she having left Ireland only recently. The Thomases took us into the town of Albany to see the capitol there, an imposing building, and just as we were being shown round Theodore Roosevelt,[4] the Governor of New York State, walked into the central hall. He happened to come in just as we entered, and without a moment's hesitation Mr Thomas spoke to a man standing near Mr Roosevelt and told him about us, whereupon we were introduced to this famous man who shook us warmly by the hand and was interested to find we had only just left England. We were astonished at his friendliness and very pleased at this unexpected introduction. After our visit to Troy we went on to see the Niagara Falls, travelling by what was then considered the fastest express in the world, namely the Empire Express to Buffalo, where we were to connect with a much slower train going to Niagara. On our arrival there we got rooms in what was considered a fairly expensive hotel which overlooked the rapids and falls, the roar of the water seemed almost deafening and we stood and gazed, almost with awe, on the majesty and beauty of the scene. The Canadian side of the falls was just as impressive. In those days the power of the falls had not been so much harnessed for commercial purposes as it is now, and the scenery was but little spoilt. After a rather sleepless night owing to the tremendous roar of the water, we went next day to the Canadian side and were taken down to the edge of the rapids formed both by the American and Canadian waters. We were allowed to stand on a spur of rock where the water flowed less rapidly over the cliffs, and were given mackintoshes and hoods to cover us well up. Where we stood we got slightly sprinkled with the water and watched the little ship, *Maid of the Mist*, on the American side taking on passengers to bring them over to our side across the swirling water. We stood on Table Rock, with mist and spray all around us, and a fog in which drops of water glittered in the sunshine. We felt indeed that this was nature at her fairest and grandest.

Next morning we left for Toronto, having paid a very steep bill at our hotel, and had a three-hour wait for the train that was to take us by Grand Trunk Railway as far as North Cape station, where we were to join the Canadian Pacific Railway and take the train to Vancouver right across the Rockies.

During our three-hour wait we went to see the new city hall of which Toronto was very proud, a very fine building not then quite finished, which put me in mind of the capitol we had so recently visited in Albany. On returning to the station we climbed into our train with quantities of hand luggage, which our fellow passengers stared at with much amusement. They had learnt to travel light with just a suitcase or two, and we soon learnt why. The sleeping car had very little space to put any packages away, and our stuff had to be stowed in various corners, most uncomfortable for everybody; we were used to much more roomy accommodation at home.

On reaching North Cape the next day, we staggered out with all our luggage and got into the Canadian Pacific train, and then began that wonderful journey across Canada. We passed Lake Windermere and skirted the shore of part of Lake Superior. We watched, fascinated with the scenery, catching occasional glimpses of wigwams, but could see no Indians. We crossed a trestle bridge said then to be the highest in Canada, and now we were well on the way to Winnipeg. We made friends with a Mr Robinson who said we should have six hours to wait when we reached Winnipeg, and he hoped we would lunch at his home during that time, after which he would drive us round the town. On arrival, however, his son met him and told him that his wife was ill, and it was arranged between father and son that we should go to lunch at the son's home. We felt that was really bad luck on the son and his wife, who did not even know us, and explained that we could not accept so kind an invitation, but they would not hear of it. So off we went, driven along log streets of which there were still a few left in Winnipeg near the station, and we arrived at the younger Mr Robinson's home. Such a pretty young woman welcomed us with a small baby in her arms. She soon gave the child over to a friendly neighbour who had come in to help, and then our hostess set herself to amuse us. After a wonderful lunch, got together for our benefit in so short a time, the Robinsons drove us round to see what were then newly laid-out streets, in a well-planned town. The wooden houses were charmingly constructed, the gardens unfenced and most attractive. I have no doubt that I should not recognise any of this town now, which has grown since then into such an enormous, prosperous commercial centre, but in those days it was still a mixture of modern and primitive. We found Mr Robinson most interested in the South African War and although very much inclined to question the motives that had first started that war, he was very loyal indeed to the mother country and anxious to help, but without sparing his criticism. We liked him greatly, and his charming wife, and were most grateful for the chance of seeing a home in Canada and to find such wonderful hospitality. We bid them goodbye hoping that perhaps sometime later we might be able to return some of their kindness should they visit England, but we never saw them again.

Our train was now passing through prairie lands, rather monotonous until we reached stations where we could stop, such as Moose Jaw where Indians met us on the platform gaily dressed, partly in their own dress and partly in European clothes. One handsome woman with her forehead heavily dyed with red was wearing loose, bright, fringed trousers, a gaudy handkerchief over her head, and then to spoil it all, a European frock coat! The men with their long plaits of hair used them to flick the flies off their faces, some wore gay coloured blankets over their shirts, and some wore wide-awake hats, and one had a moccasin on one foot and a European rubber shoe on the other. Everything European was evidently a great treasure. A friendly fellow shook Vernon by the hand, and then asked for five cents for having done so.

Back on the train, we gradually left the prairie country and entered the Rockies. Range upon range of snow-capped mountains, and hills, all densely wooded with tall pine trees, cedars and firs, and here and there mountain torrents forming beautiful cascades, and waterfalls splashing down from a great height. The rivers wound slowly in and out of rocks and chasms, we could see them from bridges three hundred feet above, or when our train ran just on the edge of the banks. Fortunately we were going pretty slowly and had ample time to take in the splendour of the scene, often from the observation car at the rear of the train. We stopped at Field, then a delightful mountain village, and had breakfast in a small chalet hotel, and at Glacier House, another exquisite mountain village, we had lunch. I felt almost in a charmed land, the sun shining and glistening on the ice-blue of the highest peak of that tremendous range, and the deep silence and grandeur all round was most awe-inspiring and the beauty and wonder of the scenery at Glacier House seemed to us the most impressive part of the whole range of the Rockies. How glad we were that there was no dining car on the train, for the last two days had given us an unexpected opportunity to get out of the train and admire the wonderful majesty of these mountain ranges.

Our next stop was Medicine Hat where many Indians stood about in their gay clothes and feathered headdresses, some of the women very pretty in spite of red dye and black stains on their faces. They persuaded us to buy some of their wretched little tomahawks especially made for visitors' souvenirs, and only an encumbrance when bought, also highly beaded moccasins. I felt I was indeed being had for a mug when I was persuaded to buy them. Later we reached Revelstoke and our train took on a dining car, much to our regret for we were no longer able to sample the little mountain hotels for meals. As we neared the western side of Canada we found the vegetation much more advanced, the mountains perhaps not quite so rugged and on the lower slopes we could see red and white flowering currant bushes blooming gaily, and even raspberry bushes fruiting well, though it was so early in the year. We were now nearing Vancouver and on May 2nd we arrived. We had greatly enjoyed that train journey, there was so much to see that we were really sad to step off the train.

Vancouver is a beautiful town overlooking the harbour, surrounded by mountains and forests, the woods skirting the many bays and inlets, and the colouring of the water and woodlands quite exquisite. From our hotel we could see an Indian village across the water, Vancouver Island in the far distance and then the snow-capped mountains rising behind the bay. We were to stay until our ship, the *Empress of China*, was ready to leave on May 8th, and make a few last-minute preparations for our voyage across the Pacific. At the shipping office they wished to know if we had been vaccinated. Rather surprised we said we had not, and were told it was essential, so that had to be fixed up and was an unnecessary precaution as neither of us responded at all. Now we had time to look around and went to the famous Victoria Park with its gigantic trees, some of them of such girth that you could drive a coach through the trunk, one such tree actually having a large archway through it. There was almost a small zoo in the park, with bears, pumas, monkeys, lynxes, vultures, lovely Chinese pheasants and many varieties of birds. We amused ourselves feeding the bears, one of which obligingly climbed a tree for us. The next couple of days were wet, and Vernon started a bout of asthma, but it did not last long. Monday being my birthday we celebrated it with a bottle of champagne, how little I thought a year ago that my twenty-first birthday would be spent here in Canada. Some papers had to be signed before a lawyer as I was now twenty-one, for they had been left incomplete before this date and could now be dealt with.

3

JAPAN

❖

On May 8th we left in the *Empress of China*, a ship reckoned quite a fair size in those days though she was only six thousand tons, but she was a very good sea boat. We sat at the captain's table; he was a charming man, very reserved and quiet, but most interesting. Our ship steamed slowly towards Vancouver Island and on reaching Victoria many of the local people came on board and seemed to take charge of the ship until they were ordered off at sailing time. Soon our ship was rolling and pitching in the Pacific and we had a very unpleasant time, and as the days passed the rolling persisted steadily and easily, but the pitching ceased and we got quite used to the motion of the ship.

We made friends with several of the passengers, especially with Mr Drummond, a banker recently married and who was expecting his wife to follow him and meet him in Shanghai. Some of the passengers were going to Japan but most of them to Shanghai and Hong Kong. Many had spent long years in the East and loved the life there. It is rather a monotonous voyage until one reaches the Japanese coast, the ocean so vast, and only a few ships to be seen passing by. It made quite an excitement to get up in the early dawn to see the Aleutian Islands, but that was a disappointment for they were shrouded in mist and were barely visible. As we neared the coast of Japan a thick fog blotted out the view and visibility was nil. The captain of our ship, a mail boat, hardly dared to slow down the ship, knowing that his headquarters at Hong Kong would expect him to bring the mail on time, thus avoiding the payment of the heavy fine that was exacted from his company should the mail be late. The currents were intensely strong, and without a certain amount of way, his ship could easily be diverted from its course. Vernon and I wondered rather nervously what would happen next and were not surprised when suddenly the ship scraped against something, and the engines were put full speed astern. Just then the fog lifted and what a sight met our eyes! We had been steaming right onto the rocky shore, no fog signals, nothing to tell us of the dangers of that part of the Japanese coast. Fortunately the rock we had scraped was flat-topped and had done no damage to the ship, as a later inspection at Yokohama confirmed. It was an amazing escape.

We reached Yokohama on the morning of May 22nd, and were entranced with the beauty of that harbour, the mountains in the distance, the lovely bays with houses nestling by the water's edge, those simple, exquisite Japanese houses, unspoilt then by European and American influence which later produced the large commercial buildings taking away so much of the beauty of the coast towns. We felt, as we landed on a sightseeing expedition, almost as if we ourselves were being pictured in those paintings that were offered for sale in the shops. Our friend Mr Drummond, who knew Yokohama well, showed us round and took us to some little shops selling silks and robes of every colour. On entering we were intended to leave our shoes on the doorstep so as not to spoil the spotless matting everywhere carpeting the floors, but being foreigners we were excused. The courtesy of the salesmen surprised us, and it was almost like a ritual making a purchase. Yokohama, even in 1900, was a port of great importance, the streets were all laid out in a regular pattern, everything so compact, and we were immensely impressed by the cleanliness of the streets, even of the poorest.

We regretfully returned to our ship; we should have loved to spend days at Yokohama, but were due to leave for Kobe in a few hours, so we waved goodbye rather sadly, for Japan was beginning to cast her spell over us. It was evening when we arrived at Kobe, and there was a golden glow over the hills, the town itself spreading out before us, gleaming with little points of light as the lamps were lit in the streets, and the rickshaws darted in and out with their little lamps swinging and shining in the darkness. We were allowed on shore for a few hours and our friend Mr Drummond took us to see what sights we could at that late hour: we hired three rickshaws and were taken at great speed by the fleet-footed coolies to the local theatre. One of the coolies became the leader and took us through some of the poorest parts of town, and again we were amazed at the neatness and cleanliness of the streets and shops. We stepped off our rickshaws to look into some of these shops and admired the artistic way the goods were displayed. I noticed in one tiny window that a little plain wooden photo frame had been made most attractive with a sprig of real ivy trailing over one side of it. Just such little touches everywhere showed the real love of beauty that is inherent in the Japanese character.

Getting back into our rickshaws we were taken along to the theatre. Again our leading coolie constituted himself our guide and did the honours of the place. A play was going on which was being acted as in real life, taking months or even years to conclude. We were led into a box, one of the only ones in that primitive theatre. It overlooked the audience on the floor of the house on which the people were all sitting, for it was spaced with little square deal partitions, rather like a huge chessboard, each person sitting in a square, with teapots and small food bowls on little trays beside them. The actors were in European dress and some of the furniture was European. A big arc light hung from the centre of the auditorium decorated with long fronds of lacy seaweed, the light it gave was sufficient for both stage and auditorium. The audience, seeing strangers come into the box, turned their back on the players who were two men facing each other without moving a muscle, each one pointing a pistol at the other, and uttering never a word. Apparently the audience found us much more interesting to look at, and stared at us till we departed, leaving the actors still facing each other in the same menacing silence. We were told that this play was a Japanese classic, and was being acted in true, traditional style. It would take many months before it was concluded, and had already taken a year or two to get to the point we had just seen. Our coolies, who were very friendly people, took us back to our ship and, wishing us a good journey, left us very well pleased with their remuneration.

Early next morning we steamed towards the Inland Sea. We came up on deck to watch the dawn breaking over the exquisite scene that met our eyes, for the pale light gleaned opalescent over the smooth iridescent waters. In the far distance we could see little fishing boats, two men in each boat who wore no clothes but wide cone-shaped hats, and were silhouetted hazily in the silvery light. These men were fishing with the aid of a cormorant perched in the bow of each boat; the bird would dive into the water and bring a fish up in its beak which would at once be taken from it, for it wore a metal ring round its neck, preventing any but the tiniest fish from being swallowed. We were too far away to watch this method of fishing, but the whole scene was beautiful in the pale dawn as our ship steamed into the Inland Sea, surely one of the loveliest in the world. As we reached the landlocked waters we found ourselves hurrying from one side of the ship to the other, trying not to miss the beauty of the coast with its picturesque villages on either side nestling in the coves and in the shelter of the hills.

When we reached Nagasaki on May 25th we were still so thrilled with the scenery we had just left that the much-fortressed harbour of Nagasaki struck a note of grimness. Its majestic hills seemed almost forbidding, the impression made the stronger in our minds by the stringent precautions taken by the local police to ensure that none of us, should we go on shore, could approach any of the many forbidden areas kept exclusively within military jurisdiction. There must be immense changes since we were there and Nagasaki more grimly fortified than ever. We were to spend a whole day here, for they were coaling our ship; rather a primitive procedure, but exceedingly quick and very efficient. Swarms of ladders were placed against the ship's sides resting on the coal barges and small baskets filled with coal were passed from hand to hand by young girls stationed at different points up these ladders. It all went at an amazing speed and we watched fascinated by this novel method of coaling ships. We left that evening and the ship pitched rather heavily as we ploughed through some heavy weather in the Yellow Sea.

4

SHANGHAI AND
ACTIVE SERVICE

❖

As we neared the mouth of the River Yangtse the water seemed to get yellower and muddier. We steamed up towards Shanghai where our ship anchored, and we were taken by small steamer up to the Bund in Shanghai. Here, after many goodbyes to our fellow passengers, we found the necessary rickshaws with the help of our friend Mr Drummond, and set out for the rooms that had been recommended to us. Now I quote from a manuscript written by Vernon:

We eventually settled on a boarding house run by an English woman and called Ka-Li, and on the following morning my Chinese teacher arrived, bowing deeply and shaking his own hands, the custom which they affect in China and which is certainly more hygienic than the European fashion. We were very comfortably installed and my Chinese lessons progressed rapidly. One of the first things my teacher had to decide on was to give me a suitable Chinese name. He could find nothing that would give the Chinese equivalent in one syllable, so he proceeded to explain that my name would be divided into two monosyllables, namely Ko-Lu, the nearest he could get to Kell. Now I heard that it was necessary to be very careful what name one accepted from the teacher, as sometimes he would give you a name in Chinese which, when translated into verbal terms, would mean something appalling. I found, however, that my teacher had chosen two very excellent characters, 'ko-lu' which means 'capable of blessing', so I felt I could not cavill with such a name, however far from the truth it might be.

I found the work very trying at first, especially endeavouring to make the Chinese characters, some of which had to be copied in strict rotation otherwise one would be sure to omit some of them. Seven weeks then passed in heavenly weather and interesting occupation, my wife spending her time in visiting the native city and endeavouring to become an expert in Chinese porcelain and in bronze vases. Towards the beginning of June the activities of a Chinese society called the I-Ho-Chuan (or Big Sword Society) became more and more evident.[1] This popular type of anti-foreign brigand society was called 'The Boxers'.[2] Rumours about it had been spreading for some time, and information coming from various sources indicated the gathering of the society under a very powerful and influential leader, who claimed miraculous powers of immortality and invulnerability for himself and his followers. Their main professed object was against foreigners in general and Christians in particular, but brigandage and looting were also among their powerful objectives.

To digress for a moment, I must explain that we had at this time in Wei-Hai-Wei (a place which had been leased to us by the Chinese) a Chinese regiment recruited entirely from the Chinese under the leadership of British officers, a very fine and loyal regiment which did very excellent and creditable work during the Boxer Campaign which was about to open. It was commanded by Lt Colonel Hamilton-Bower, a Scotsman, explorer and a fine leader of men.[3] His second in command was a Major CD Bruce, a great explorer and traveller in China and Tibet. As soon as the Boxer threat became apparent Colonel Dorward, RE[4] was ordered up to Tientsin and Admiral Seymour dispatched in his flagship to Taku; between them they were to form a naval and military expedition for the relief of Peking.[5] As soon as I heard of the possibilities of an expedition being formed to proceed north to Tientsin and Peking I wired to Colonel Dorward, 'Here I am, take me,' and offered my services in any capacity. Norwood wired back, 'Come up by the next boat.' It is easy to imagine my delight at being ordered up on active service, especially after I had had the mortification of seeing my regiment off to South Africa to the Boer War.

The only fly in the ointment was the fact that I had to leave my wife alone in Shanghai, with the hope that she might later be given leave to follow me at any *rate as far as Wei-Hai-Wei. The next few days were employed in a hectic rush to buy what kit I could collect, as I had no uniform with me. By the end of the week I had got together a very motley kind of half-civilian kit and with this proceeded on board the last ship to leave Shanghai for the north, laden to the gunwales with stores, cattle and ammunition for the troops. About three others and I were the only passengers on board. The captain, a Russian, was fortunately a very nice man and we were a happy little community. We were lucky in the weather as otherwise I don't believe we could ever have reached port, we were so heavily laden. We arrived off the Taku Bar four days after leaving Shanghai. I was not sorry as the food on board left much to be desired and my cabin was full of cockroaches. A tug came off to meet us and took off some of our stuff, which was urgently needed for Tientsin, and we proceeded up the Pei Ho River towing some barges laden with pom-poms and maxims. The river was a nasty mud colour, with dead bodies of Chinese floating down at intervals. I arrived in Tientsin in the middle of the siege on the Fourth of July, American Independence Day, and reported myself to Colonel Dorward. He said with a smile that now I had come he did not know what to do with me, but at any rate, for a start, he would make me his ADC and Russian interpreter to the Forces.[6]*

Before leaving England some cousins of mine told me that a certain Sidney Barton, a great friend of theirs, was somewhere in China, and if I met him would I give him all kinds of messages. I thought this was rather a tall order, seeing as China is not exactly a small country to find an individual in! Strangely enough, the first man into whose room I was ushered to have a wash and brush-up was Sidney Barton (Barton, years afterwards, became our first Minister to Abyssinia).[7] He said to me, 'Come away from that corner, as the Chinese are sniping at us from that direction.' Our headquarters had been established rather foolishly in a large and conspicuous building with a dome roof forming a very easy target for the Chinese to aim at. As I was coming down the main staircase after tea that afternoon a shrapnel shell burst on the building and came down in a shower of bullets all over the stairs, fortunately missing me, how I do not know. One of our staff, Lieut Browne, RE, who was having his bath in the hall at the foot of the stairs, was also showered upon and wounded in the foot. He hopped out and held the bath up to show me it was riddled like a sieve.

The next day whilst we were having lunch, a pom-pom shell came in through the ceiling and went straight through the dining table between a staff officer and myself, fortunately exactly in the middle, without touching either of us, and did not explode. After that, Colonel Dorward thought it wisest to remove our headquarters to some safe and less conspicuous place. A Mr Cousins, the representative of the firm of Jardine Matheson, offered his house and business premises which we were very pleased to accept. Five of us staff officers slept on the floor in one large room and made ourselves comparatively comfortable.

Dorward's original staff now consisted of:

Colonel Menzies	*Chief of Staff*
Captain Borrett RN[8]	*Naval Staff Officer*
Mr Sidney Barton	*Chinese Interpreter*
Myself	*ADC and Russian Interpreter*

End of Vernon's account.

5

BOXER REBELLION

❧

L eft alone in my rooms at Ka-Li I looked out of my large veranda onto the busy streets and watched the coolies passing to and fro with their curious barrows filled with large packets of merchandise. They made an incessant din with their loud chattering voices and the squeaking of their barrow wheels. These barrows were fitted with a large centre wheel with short wooden planks on either side to hold the packages, and passing from the barrow handles over the coolies' shoulders was a big wide band of leather enabling the coolies to balance the immense weights they carried. Occasionally they took passengers as well as goods, and then a nice adjustment of weights was necessary. Blue-robed little women with feet pressed into shoes about five and a half inches long were often to be seen sitting balanced on one of these creaking barrows; they were glad of a lift as they could not walk far on their tiny feet. Of course, many years later the squeezed foot was no longer thought necessary, it was even frowned on, as education and modern ideas took root. But when we were there all Chinawomen had the bound feet except those who worked in the fields and theirs were extraordinarily small.

Looking at the blue-robed crowd, for all the coolies wore the blue cotton robe, I wondered if all these people had the intense hatred of the foreigner that was being worked up everywhere, or whether some would be loyal to us, as indeed, later on, so many of them proved to be.

Before leaving Shanghai, Vernon had called on Mr Little, editor of the *North China Herald*, who immediately took a great interest in him, especially as he knew that Vernon had been asked, before he left London, to be a correspondent for the *Daily Telegraph*. His wife, who came to see us, introduced us to the famous country club in the Bubbling Well Road where the lovely gardens and tennis courts attracted all the fashionable people of Shanghai. She became quite a friend and would chat gaily about everything except the one thing that was making everyone anxious and apprehensive, namely the news of Chinese anti-foreign activity, both in and around Shanghai and at Peking. We were constantly hearing of how the Boxers were succeeding with alarming swiftness to poison the minds of the villagers and townsmen, thus creating a very perilous situation for all foreigners. These latter were traders of many nations, bankers, officials, people residing peacefully, and gainfully employed, who up to then trusted the Chinese people absolutely. The Chinese in return had respected them and worked for them, satisfied with the prosperity it brought them. Now, however, something had to be done, and steps to try and insure protection and defence had to be taken. A volunteer force was enrolled at Shanghai and anyone with military experience was welcome.

While Vernon was still in Shanghai we had met Colonel Bower's sister-in-law, Mrs Bullard, for his wife was staying with her waiting for the chance to take her tiny baby back to Wei-Hai-Wei where she had a delightful little house. She had lived very happily there while her husband was commanding the Chinese regiment and she hoped that though Colonel Bower would now probably be at Tientsin, she could go and wait for him there, little realising how impossible that would be as the Boxer War proceeded. When Colonel Bower had suggested to Vernon that he should join Colonel Dorward's staff, if required, I had listened with deep misgivings and, truth to tell, rather alarmed at the prospect of being left alone in such strange surroundings. But I was much more terrified at what might happen to Vernon, for scare stories of all sorts were being spread about of the tortures and brutalities committed on those who had the misfortune to fall into the hands of the Boxers, and we know that some of these stories were only too true.

Vernon felt sure that all the people we had already met in Shanghai would continue to show the wonderful hospitality we had already received, and Colonel Bower had greatly eased his mind by telling him that his sister-in-law would see that I was all right and could come to her in any difficulty. Just before he left, the news had come through of the murder of the German minister at Peking, the Boxers were gaining in strength and we were told that the legations were besieged.[1] To add to that, we heard that regular troops of the Chinese Army were assisting the Boxers; they had been ordered to do so by the Empress Dowager who was turning the Boxer rising to good account to forward her own ambitions, for she desired to be absolute ruler of the Chinese, and to force out the foreigners.[2] There was but little means of defence for these legations, just a very high wall surrounded them and this could easily be made a point of vantage for the Boxers who were erecting platforms for the use of their snipers. At some distance from the legations stood the famous Peitang Cathedral and we heard that nuns, monks and Chinese christians of all sorts, had taken refuge there, for the Boxers were ill-treating and torturing any foreigner they could find including any Chinese who had served them. We were told that literally hundreds of people in the cathedral, living under dreadfully unsanitary conditions, were starving, and children and old people lay there dying and dead, the nuns trying heroically to relieve the horror of it all. Tales of massacres and torture kept on pouring in, and we heard that no food whatever could now get through to the legations, no one could step outside the buildings without becoming an immediate target for the snipers watching from the platforms outside the walls. We knew that the Boxers were massing together to enable them to take the legations by force of numbers, and, but of the fact that these forces were very badly armed, mostly with very antiquated weapons, it would never have been possible to relieve the legations in time. The English had sent a naval column from Her Majesty's ships at Wei-Hai-Wei under Admiral Seymour which had just gone up by road towards Peking from Taku, the port nearest to Tientsin.[3]

But it was a very small contingent and quite inadequately equipped to meet the sort of guerrilla forces that they were to encounter. Sickness and fever struck down many of the men, and from what we could hear the column was making very little headway, and transport of sick and wounded made the pace very slow. We knew that eventually we should reach Peking when adequate forces arrived to give us the means, but there was always the desperate fear that the relief might be too late. Vernon had gone off to Tientsin with no uniform, not even a khaki sunhat, and I had horrid fears of sunstroke to add to those for his safety. However, I hoped things would turn out all right for him; they had a way of doing that, I thought.

I had wondered what I had better do now on my own, but was not left long in doubt. A message came from Mrs Bullard, Mrs Bower's sister, that I must go straight away to stay with her till Vernon's return, as she said it was quite unthinkable that I should live alone at Ni-Kalee in my flat. I was only too glad of the chance of being with so nice a family and in a very large house like the Bullard's. No sooner had I received and accepted this invitation so hospitably given, than other similar invitations poured in even from people I had never met. All said that it would not be possible, under the present circumstances, for me to live alone in my flat for the ill-disposed Chinese were working up hostility to the foreigners in every way they could in the native city of Shanghai, and though the majority of the Chinese were against this, they dared not show it too openly. Guns were trained in the direction of the foreign settlements and the situation was strained and tense.

I left my flat with much relief, for I had never liked it, and I arrived at Mrs Bullard's house where a very warm welcome awaited me. This house was very comfortable and well run, the Chinese servants absolutely loyal, and there was a very nice garden and a lovely cool veranda overlooking it. In the shelter of the veranda hung a little cage and in it a tiny brown owl, a pet belonging to Mrs Bower. Thinking she would give it an airing, she put it on the lawn in the sun which of course meant that it could not see at all and it was not even in the cage. A strange thing followed; a lovely little green singing bird flew excitedly over the little owl, and immediately a whole chorus of brightly coloured birds came swooping down nearer and nearer to the helpless little owl till I realised that the birds were calling to each other from all directions and meant to peck it to death. It had to be speedily rescued, and never again while I was in China did I see such lovely birds of every colour and size. It was a mystery to me where they could have come from.

While I stayed with Mrs Bullard we lived the ordinary social life of Shanghai, tinged with deep anxiety especially when we heard the most disquieting news of the naval relief column under Admiral Seymour. It was being driven back, for they were quite unprepared to find the Boxers in such strength, reinforced as they were by worked-up mobs of Chinese villagers who, though ill-armed, could press back our little force by sheer weight of numbers. Many of our sick and wounded sailors were sent back by slow and painful stages to our naval hospital at Liu-Ku-Tao, the island at Wei-Hai-Wei. We knew things were getting desperate, especially for the legations, but we could get little authentic news of them. In the meantime the authorities at home and in America, also in France, Germany, Russia, Austria and Italy, had ordered preparations to be made to send out contingents from each country to form a small army to relieve the legations and protect other European settlements should they need it. But these contingents took time to equip and ship out to China, and we waited strained and anxious. The papers at home were giving accounts of all this and my people became alarmed at what might be the fate that awaited Vernon and me, for our reassuring letters took so long to reach them. In desperation they sent a cable telling us to return at once before it was too late. They did not realise that had we tried to return we should probably have met more dangers than by staying where we were, and fortunately they did not know that Vernon had been called up for duty till much later on.

Days went by and still no news of Peking, but we heard that the forces from the various nations were on their way and India would be the first to land an adequate force from our Indian Army there, which would be under the command of General Gaselee.[4]

6

RELIEF OF PEKING

❧

I
t was now very hot in Shanghai and Mrs Bower and I tried to find some shipping accommodation to take us to Wei-Hai-Wei, where it would be much cooler, and Mrs Bower hoped to go back to her home. Vernon had arranged before he went to Tientsin to take rooms in the island of Liu-Kun-Tao close to Wei-Hai-Wei, and we had booked them for the months of July and August. Our naval and military headquarters had their official residences and offices at Liu-Kun-Tao, where there was also quite a thriving community of Chinese. Accommodation for visitors was rather meagre but we had booked early.

Mrs Bower and I heard of a small cargo boat going north, and we decided to travel in her, my intention being to go to the rooms Vernon had reserved for me. We started off on July 11th in that very small ship laden to the gunwale with cargo and merchandise of all sorts. Mrs Bower had brought some rattan easy chairs to put in her house and they were dumped on the deck. We found them most useful and hoped they would keep steady, for we sat uncommonly near the water, our ship being dangerously overloaded. I helped with the baby as there was no amah for her, the one in Shanghai having refused to travel north. I said goodbye most regretfully to the Bullards who have been so wonderfully good to me, and we never met again.

It was a flat calm all the way to Wei-Hai-Wei. We spent those two days of lovely weather mostly sitting on the deck, for our cabins were the smallest imaginable, the roof nearly touching our heads as we lay in our bunks, and stuffy beyond description. We reached our destination on July 13th and were met by a launch that had been sent to meet Mrs Bower. I was evidently taken to be the nanny, for I was holding the baby for Mrs Bower, and got safely on shore little knowing that no one was being allowed on Liu-Kun-Tao Island except those notified to the resident, General Dorward, and his staff. Mrs Bower was told that it was not considered safe for her to live on Wei-Hai-Wei mainland where her husband's official house was, for she would have been the only white woman there. Colonel Bower's brother officers, who helped him to raise the Chinese regiment, were all now on active service and fighting their way towards the relief of Peking. There was only one other officer's wife left, a friend of Mrs Bower's and she had also been sent, for greater safety, to live on the island. I now got off to look for our rooms only to find that these had been allotted to the Bishop of Peking's wife, a Mrs Scott, and no place could be found for me.[1] How had I landed and why? Who had given permission? There was much head scratching, and it was realised that as the nanny I had landed without any hindrance. That was fortunate, otherwise I should have been ordered to return to my destination in Shanghai with no money to pay my fare. My troubles were not yet at an end, for no accommodation could be found for me, and eventually after a very uncomfortable shake-down for the night I was given a room which Mrs Bower and her baby shared with me. This would only be quite temporary, they said, for which we were thankful, for it was getting very hot and one small room was pretty close quarters. Maude Bower was a delightful companion and made light of all her discomforts; she said that, whatever happened, we should share digs when she, as colonel's wife, would be able to have them.

HMS *Terrible* was anchored in the harbour, and the famous Captain Scott in command,[2] but the actual harbour was commanded by Admiral Gaunt.[3] Commander Jellicoe was staying at the naval resident's house, on sick leave, badly wounded in the elbow; we hoped soon to meet him.[4] A naval officer's wife, who had a whole house to herself, offered me a spare room till I could get other quarters, so off I went to her for a couple of nights. When at last living quarters were found for Maude Bower and me, we settled in with great relief. Letters were now beginning to arrive from Vernon and Colonel Bower. Vernon described the action against the arsenal, not far from Tientsin, which led to the taking of the native city. There was some very heavy firing at a bridge close by, the range calculated most accurately by the Chinese attacking in the city, and as he crossed Vernon saw the man in front of him hit, and then the man directly behind him rolled over the bridge and yet Vernon was quite untouched. This was his third wonderful escape – he seemed to have a charmed life, and I cheered up on hearing he was getting on alright.

It was towards the end of July that we heard that a considerable number of troops from India had arrived, though many more were needed before a start to relieve Peking could be made. The Japanese were cooperating with us with great willingness, the Russians not nearly so easily, the French contingent was expected shortly, also the German, Italian and American contingents. The authorities decided to press on and early in August sent all the troops they could muster towards Peking.

Our island of Liu-Kun-Tao had now quite a large field unit of Indian troops stationed there, and their small base post office made us feel a little more in touch with what was going on to bring this strange Boxer War to an end. The news coming through to us was good and our forces, now better equipped and much larger, were meeting with success. I knew, of course, that Vernon was not with the relief column, but was still at headquarters in Tientsin. Every day the weather was getting hotter, and the hope was that the heavy rains expected at this time of year would not delay the relieving troops too much. There was a fear, and a deadly one, that the legations might not be able to hold out. Sir Claude MacDonald, our Minister at Peking, his wife, and all the British people who had taken refuge in the legations would, we were sure, hold on to the bitter end, but we knew they were terribly short of food and that there must be such sickness owing to the many refugees crowded into them.[5]

One awful day it was given out that the legations had been taken by the Boxers; the London papers, even *The Times*, published it, but not the *Daily Telegraph*. Vernon was still correspondent for this paper and he waited for confirmation before cabling to them. He got an indignant message from their London office but was later fully justified, and rejoicing, when on August 15th they knew that the relief forces had reached Peking just in time. The first troops had managed to trickle through those great surrounding walls at the water gate, and strangely enough the first person to get through the gate was an officer in the Indian Army called Scott. He turned out to be a cousin of mine, Edwin Thomas Scott, who later became a very distinguished general and later on was, for some time, Governor of Aden.[6] He and Vernon met at Tientsin, and being told that Vernon's wife was a Scott, discovered the relationship, and we were to see much of him a few months later. He was a witty and delightful Irishman.

I heard few details of the relief until some of the senior officers came back to General Dorward's headquarters on our island, for letters came very fitfully with long gaps in between. It was now August 26th, and there had been several moves in our little community. Mrs Scott, the Anglican Bishop's wife, had managed to get herself conveyed back to Tientsin, and Maude Bower and I were still without news of any efforts to get us out of the island or of our husbands being able to come there. Day after day passed and still no news. There were rumours: one that our troops had gone into the interior of China to try and find the Emperor and the Empress Dowager, that forceful woman who was the cause of most of the troubles that had led to the Boxer War. It was now September, and at last Vernon wrote that he had been appointed Intelligence Officer on General Lorne Campbell's staff. The latter had now taken over command of the British contingent in Tientsin, which was almost entirely composed of Indian Army units. Apparently Colonel Bower had been given some important post, we did not know exactly what it was, and both he and Vernon said they thought we could soon join them and come to Tientsin as soon as a ship came our way.

The whole International Expeditionary Force[7] consisting of contingents from eight nations had now been placed under the command of General Waldersee,[8] the German Commander-in-Chief, for the Germans had arrived in quite considerable force accompanied by heavy guns, heavy wagons and large carts quite unsuitable for the bad, narrow roads which they had to negotiate in North China. The French and Italians had much lighter and more suitable transport, except in the big town where the wide roads did not worry them. The narrow tortuous roads in the country away from the towns were impossible for any but the lightest mountain gun transport to travel on. The forces of the eight nations concerned made a pretty formidable army, as I saw for myself when I reached Tientsin. The largest forces were supplied by five nations, namely France, Russia, Japan, Germany and the British. On September 15th, while still at Liu-Kun-Tao, I got a telegram from Vernon saying he was arriving the next day, and sure enough the hospital ship *Carthage* came into the harbour, and Vernon landed in a small boat. My joy at his arrival was rather dampened when I found he was on sick leave, having contracted a sort of dysentery very common in North China. He came to our digs that night, and the tales he had to tell were fascinating. I could hardly believe he was ill for he neither looked nor felt it, but the next day the doctor ordered him into hospital where he was kept very quiet, and visits even from his wife were strictly regulated according to the red tape of military hospitals. Being a fervent Irish rebel, I could not see any reason for these rules that seemed to me to be produced for the doctors' and nurses' sole benefit. Of course some were perhaps for the patient's benefit, but I was in no mood to think so for Vernon was not ill enough to enable me to see that these rules might be useful. At last, after about six days, he was allowed back to our quarters.

Letters were now arriving from Colonel Bower with suggestions for his wife to join him as soon as he knew what his plans were. General Dorward, having just returned to our island, told us that Colonel Bower was to stay in Tientsin and would be made one of the Provisional Governors who would be appointed from the Japanese, Russian, German and French forces. It all sounded very interesting, and as Vernon was now signed off the sick list, we had only to wait to hear of a ship to take us all off to

Tientsin. We started packing up, and having heard that possibly a P&O transport would visit Wei-Hai-Wei we knew that we might get shipped off at a moment's notice. It was now September 26th and on the morning of the 30th, while we were still in bed, we heard General Dorward's voice shouting to us to hurry up as the *Dalhousie* was just entering the harbour and we should all have to be on board by lunchtime. Well we got there somehow, scrambling through our final packing, and then after all the hustle the ship did not leave till the following morning at dawn!

But now, at last, we could go north and our waiting was at an end.

7

TIENTSIN

❧

The sea was rather rough and as usual I felt squeamish, though the others were alright and enjoying the trip. Next day we arrived at Taku-Bar and missed the tug that was to have taken us over the Bar; that meant waiting on board till the next day. Colonel Bower had come to meet us, and we were greatly excited at the prospect of reaching Tientsin. A funny little tug boat, Japanese manned, arrived to take us off the ship; she looked a crazy little craft and we found her pretty crazily captained too, for when we started off towards the river mouth we nearly collided with another small ship. However, we steamed safely up the Pei-Ho river towards the stopping place at Tongku railway station, noting on the way the really strong-looking forts that would have taken our forces much longer to subdue, had they been better manned and equipped. The countryside all round us was desperately flat with no cover whatever for troops, the only elevations being the many mounds made by the Chinese when they bring their dead and leave the coffins on top of the ground, earthed up into little hills, some much bigger than others, the more imposing having a few straggly-looking trees to mark some special family burial grounds. A few mud-coloured houses were still left intact, though many others were in ruins, for a good deal of fighting had taken place close to the forts and near the river. All the junks in the river flew ensigns of the different nations that had sent ships and troops to the rescue of the legations. It certainly was a curious sight and gave

49

a feeling of security to those Chinese who were loyal to us, and were still very mindful of what might have happened had 'the foreigners', as we were called, not been successful in fighting the Boxers. On arrival at Tongku railway station all arrangements were made for our transport to Tientsin. We were surrounded by Russian, French and German soldiers, also a few Chinamen who were slowly regaining confidence in our ability to safeguard them, for they had been dubbed 'number two foreigners' by the Boxers, who had killed with great cruelty those unable to get away.

Vernon took us into the station waiting room and introduced me to Russian tea made in a samovar, and very good it was: no milk but a slice of lemon, sugar and sometimes a spoonful of jam put into the glass in which it was served. Outside were Cossack soldiers riding thin, strong and rather fiery little ponies, also droshkies stood waiting to drive away the Russian passengers, many of them women and children, evidence of the large Russian contingent which had come to this part of the fighting zone and meant to make a long stay.

On our train journey to Tientsin we could see all the havoc wrought by the bitter fighting: houses in ruins, bridges damaged and hastily repaired, and, as we neared Tientsin itself, even greater devastation. The east arsenal was entirely wrecked, the Russian and the French Concessions nearly so, and standing in the ruined station were locomotives now just a heap of scrap iron – for the fighting had been worse there than anywhere else.

As we stepped out of the train we were met and shepherded to the house of Mr Cousins where Vernon was staying, for he was kindly putting us all up till we could find other accommodation. We were hoping to share a house with the Bowers if we could find one, and in the meanwhile settled down very comfortably owing to Mr Cousin's hospitality. He told us stories of the siege of Tientsin and of the awful plague of flies that invaded them; he described how the godowns storing sugar had been set on fire, and as the sugar boiled it came down in streams of syrup all along the streets, attracting black clouds of flies that penetrated everywhere. When people sat at meals the food was smothered with them; they had to blow off the flies and quickly eat each mouthful, hoping not to swallow many of them! Small wonder that so many people suffered from fevers and dysentery in consequence.

Our British headquarters was now housed in the big temperance hall overlooking the ornamental gardens of the town, and there the damage had been very extensive from the heavy shelling. Soon after the siege of the foreign concessions was over, and the fighting had all died down after the native city had been taken, the Boxers themselves made abortive stands well away from the big towns and then seemed to disappear. Vernon had much to tell me and I insert here his account of his visit to Peking where he had been before I had joined him in Tientsin:

> The first day I spent in the legation grounds looking round all the old defences, and was shown the various hot corners during the siege. It was really wonderful how those people managed to hold out so long. I also went to see the Roman Catholic Cathedral called the 'Pehtang', which was relieved after the legations. It was a strange sight to go into this ruined building still crammed with Chinese converts, of whom many had been killed. Seventy-six children were blown up by the explosion of a mine, and ten French marines and five Italians had been buried within the walls. For the last month these poor people had been down to four ounces of rice a day, and during the last week of the siege they had been reduced to two ounces. How glad they were to see us! Poor Archbishop Favier, with tears in his eyes, gave us a description of all the horrors – far worse than our own – that they had been through.[1] From the time that Baron Ketteler was killed on June 20th to the time that a Japanese officer marched into the cathedral on August 15th to tell them that relief was at hand, they had heard no news of any description.[2]
>
> I went myself to see the large crater formed by the mine that the Chinese exploded in trying to undermine the cathedral; it was about twenty feet deep and thirty feet across. The next day we drove out in a tonga, a light Indian cart, to the Summer Palace, about twelve miles out in the country – a lovely place, all the more interesting because there are but few people who have seen it. I believe it was visible in 1860, after the war. There was nothing very much to see inside these places, as most of the valuables had been looted, but we now had a guard to watch over a very large room full of various priceless things, mostly cloisonné

ware, and gold elephants, etc, and clocks by the hundred, some with mechanical figures. We saw some wonderful temples, one built entirely of porcelain, another of bronze, and there too was a paddleboat made entirely of marble. The whole grounds are beautifully situated in the western hills, the scenery perfectly lovely. A huge lake frozen over now in the winter gave an opportunity for splendid skating to the 'Foreign Devils', also there was good duck shooting. Not a single portable thing was left anywhere in the palace, all cleared by the looters, which seemed barbarous behaviour on the part of the troops.

We had started from Peking at 9.15am and got to the palace at 10.45. Rather good going in a tonga. The road was paved the whole way from the city walls, the Emperor and the Empress and their suites being the only people who ever used that route to the Summer Palace. We drove back to Peking, having been nearly upset into a deep ditch owing to our lively tonga ponies, which had been sent out the night before to bring us back. The next day I joined a party of officers to view the Forbidden City, which was strictly guarded by Japanese and Americans, passes being required to see the place. I must say it is very disappointing. It must have been very fine about three or four hundred years ago, but now the walls and buildings looked rather dilapidated. The throne room was very fine, especially the ceiling, but the dirt and filth inside was awful, even in the Emperor's bedroom. The finest things there were the marble slabs and steps leading up to all the various inner courts and halls, also the bronze lions that adorned the entrances of all the courtyards. On our way back we met Major Scott, a cousin of my wife's, and we went curio hunting. I spent a fortune but all in good bargains, for I had a connoisseur with me. Nearly all the wares displayed on little stalls in the streets were stolen and looted by the Chinese, who did not know their value, and we struck some good bargains. I brought these treasures back to Tientsin and hoped we might soon have a house where we could show off some really beautiful specimens of Chinese art.

While Vernon and I stayed at Mr Cousin's house we met many well-known people, amongst others Colonel Grierson, the English representative attached to the German Commander-in-Chief staff.[3] He had been a great friend of Kaiser William,[4] and was a very fine linguist, a most interesting man who had just come from South Africa where he was on Lord Roberts' staff.[5] Another was Maharajah Bikanir, who was then very young and extraordinarily good-looking, a friend of Queen Victoria's.[6] It was easy to see why she had taken such an interest in him for he was a true courtier. An excellent painting of him was presented to her, and some years later I saw it in Buckingham Palace, he looking just as I remembered him in Tientsin. Again very many years later our daughter, just grown up, had gone with Lady Birdwood, wife of our Commander-in-Chief, India, to stay at the Rajah's palace as guests in one of the big parties assembled to take part in his famous shoots.[7] It seemed strange that we should have met him in China, where many other well known Rajahs had also come with their regiments, people such as Sir Pertab Singh,[8] and Rajah Gwalior.[9] Sir Pertab was most beloved by all who knew him in India; he was brave, high principled and a wonderful sportsman. He appealed especially to the British, who had an enormous admiration for him.

Vernon was now meeting many of the local residents, people who had gone through the dangers and hardships of the siege with great bravery. They were all so cheerful and made all the newcomers welcome. Colonel Bower, now one of the Provisional Governors of the native city of Tientsin, was looking everywhere for a house for his family which we could share with him. He heard of one quite nice one but the present owner had let it get into a very derelict condition, for it was dirty, untidy and generally pretty uncomfortable, and was undecided whether to continue living there or not, but eventually he agreed to leave the house. Just before this Vernon had to leave Tientsin and join a small punitive force sent to Pao-Ting-Pu, which was far up country. He was, of course, looking forward to it, for it would give him some more experience and be interesting. The weather was fine and sleeping out in the open would be pleasant, and in October he went off, not returning till well on in November. In the meanwhile we moved into the rather dismal house, which was to be our home for many months. It had received a good deal of punishing from the guns of both the arsenal and the native city, bits of shrapnel and bullets had smashed many windows, but it had no structural damage. The day we moved in was a snowy day, very cold, and all the broken windows made it more miserable than ever. The house was covered with dust, and our rain-soaked feet turned the dust on the floors to mud, it took days of cleaning and clearing to get it into some sort of order. I was glad that Vernon was away, for there was hope that we should get things a bit straighter by the time he returned. I might say that far from sharing the house with the Bowers I found they were paying for everything and we were really their guests; they were quite wonderful hosts and would not hear of our paying for anything.

Tientsin was now recovering from the effects of the siege and was settling down to enjoy the gaiety of the very cosmopolitan society of its citizens. The Indian Army contingents stationed there provided us with bands to play in the public gardens, there was polo to watch, and as for dinners and lunches they were numberless. We met French, Germans, Russians, Italians, Japanese and some Americans; it was intensely interesting especially to those who could speak their languages.

On Vernon's return from the Poa-Ting-Fu expedition he made friends with many of them, knowing their languages except Japanese. It was a joyful day when he arrived back and he had much to tell, for the punitive mission was successful, the influential Chinese of the district had proved quite co-operative and there had been no actual fighting.

It was indeed a unique experience to be in Tientsin at that time, living in the east and yet surrounded by really interesting people belonging to so many different European nations. Amongst the Russian community we met a colonel in a line regiment who went about accompanied by his two daughters, two very round-about ladies who never seemed to speak, but smiled rather fatuously at people when introduced to them. There was also a Russian general always immaculately turned out who was in the Tsar's entourage; he was a man of keen intelligence, possessed of a very sharp tongue, and it was as well to be careful when talking to him. One of the people we met and liked most was a certain Colonel Aoki, who was the Japanese Provisional Governor of Tientsin, one of the five who ruled the native city. Colonel Aoki often came to dine with us and on one occasion he discussed the three days' looting which had been officially permitted in the city as part of the punishment for the fighting against the foreign concessions. He said his soldiers had been strictly forbidden to loot, as it was most demoralising, but he had instructed them to go into the native banks and take the bars of silver stored in the vaults. These he sent straight off to Japan, explaining that Japan needed the money for she was a poor country. It was true enough that the Japanese soldiers were extraordinary well disciplined. Colonel Aoki had a great admiration of the British, he was a man of deep sincerity and charm, and Colonel Bower liked him best of all the Provisional Governors he had to work with. Japan was then a friendly, kindly country; the Western merchant spirit had not yet changed her outlook, nor given a chance to adventurers who did not keep to her honourable ways.

Vernon was now appointed temporarily to be Railway Staff Officer at Tientsin, which gave him interesting work where his languages were in constant request as interpreter.

8

VISIT TO TANGSHAN

❖

I t was in December of that year, towards the end of the month, that
disquieting rumours of Queen Victoria's health reached us, and in
January we realised that she would not recover. On the 22nd we were
told of her death. We could hardly conceive of England, our empire,
without our queen – she seemed the personification of all we held dear.
Now, for a time, everything seemed turned into mourning and uneasy
forebodings, strange it should affect us all so tremendously when we were
so far from home. But that was no exaggeration, we felt rudderless for
quite a long time. There was a service, a commemoration funeral service,
held on the racecourse at Tientsin as so many people from the nations
represented there would be present, and detachments from their various
troops. General Waldersee, the Commander-in-Chief, was in command.
It was an intensely cold day and while the service was still proceeding
a dust storm came up, and sand blown straight from the Gobi Desert
covered us with mud as the rain soaked us. The wind was piercingly
cold and blew fiercely, and we were thankful when the impressive service
ended and we could hurry home. We took off our coats, which were
impregnated with the dust, driven in hard by the wind and rain, and
we could not use them again till they had been beaten like a carpet and
shaken fit to tear them, and in spite of our efforts they never looked clean
again. We dreaded those Gobi Desert dust storms, they made us feel quite
dried up like a piece of parchment. People's nerves were none the better

for all this drying up; it was so depressing, and made many people feel really ill, others became irritable beyond bearing.

Vernon and I were now taking steps to find a house for ourselves as we did not want to trespass too long on the kindness of the Bowers. At last we heard of one furnished, quite small, with a domestic staff at our disposal; we could take this one for some months. By the spring we were in it and Maude Bower had by then left for England, and her husband had to go to Peking leaving the rather desolate house we had been living in. We missed them greatly, they had done so much to help us when we were in such difficulties at first in Shanghai and again in Tientsin. But on Mrs Bower's return from England they lived too far away from us in Peking and it was impossible to meet.

There was a flurry for a time when General Gazelle, our Commander-in-Chief, decided that it was inadvisable to have any soldiers' wives out in North China and that therefore those who were already there, such as myself, must go home. General Campbell, in command in Tientsin, sent his ADC round to tell me of this, but I could not see his point, as I had come out with Vernon before the fighting, when his intention was to study Chinese to get the interpretership. I felt my case was different, and though I was told that I should be creating a precedent, I remained quite unprepared to carry out what I thought was most unjust. My contention was strengthened when a certain Captain Hume and his wife and sister arrived in Tientsin, for they too were not subject to the orders of the General, Captain Hume having come out independently. Eventually I was left alone and in peace, rather to the amusement of Vernon who laughingly wondered how I was going to get out of doing what the General wished.

It was now April 5th and we had been married for a whole eventful year. So much had happened in that time, it seemed ages since we had left Ireland. Vernon was kept very hard at work and during the winter he had several rather sharp attacks of asthma owing to the intense cold, but they had not bothered him much. He was enjoying his varied work, meeting so many most interesting people of many nationalities and our house was constantly in request as a rendezvous, especially at teatime or for dinner. Our house boy, a very experienced servant, negotiated all our many entertainments most efficiently and we had no bother, except to find the money to pay the bills! However, Vernon's staff pay was a boon, we had not reckoned on that when we came out, meaning to live on his meagre lieutenant's pay supplemented by a very modest private income, which went nowhere when we got to China. It was curious, as time went on, to find that at no stage in Vernon's subsequent career was he ever anything else but on the staff, never rejoining his regiment, for he was continuously appointed to special jobs.

Vernon was ordered off now to take over temporarily the duties of the Railway Staff Officer at Tongku station, a most important one not far from the port of Taku. Major Dunsterville, who had been posted there as one of our most able officers who could speak Russian fluently and was a really fine linguist, had to go on sick leave for a short time and Vernon was to do his work.[1] Major Dunsterville was the hero of Kipling's *Stalky & Co* though few people realised that.[2] Tongku station was a meeting place for the different military authorities of the many nations concerned in the fighting. It was so near the port of entry that it was essential that a really good linguist should be in charge of the station. Vernon went off there leaving me to look after a young American girl, Miss Henry, who was staying with us and was most charming and gay. She and I had a delightful invitation to stay in Mr Kinder's house in Tangshan, a good way up the railway line on the way to Shan-Hai-Kuan (now known as Shan-Hai-Guan) which we eagerly accepted and arrived at his lovely comfortable house. Our hostess, the Japanese wife of Mr Kinder, was a sweet and gracious little lady who interested us greatly. Her husband, Mr Kinder, had originally gone out to China with a few picked engineers, and had got the first contract to build a railway in North China. His railway engine was almost the replica of the 'Rocket', and the Chinese were most suspicious of this fire-belching devil and inclined to consider it could bring them harm, but by dint of good wages and fair dealing Mr Kinder and his team won their confidence and the railway was built. It ran from Tongku to Tientsin, from there on to Peking, and from Tientsin, a branch line, ran through Tangshan to Shan-Hai-Kuan and Newchuang. The earliest portion was the one near Tangshan on account of its coalmines, which were run by a mining company in which an American, a Mr Hoover, was greatly interested.[3] He was my American friend's brother-in-law.

Mr Kinder spent a couple of days at his house while we were staying there. He was a most delightful man who had raised England's prestige very high in China by building the railway and bringing much trade to the north. He had married a lovely little Japanese girl when he first went out to the east as a young man and she loved him with an adoration that never ceased. He tried to educate her and teach her English ways and ideas, she read many of our young girls' story books, but he could not get past the complete want of education of Japanese and Chinese girls customary in those days, even amongst the best families. This gentle, simple Japanese girl asked for nothing more than to keep his love and give him all the devotion of which she was capable. He was a very clever, very remarkable man who needed companionship badly, and though he remained loyal to her always she could not fill the place he offered her in his life and both were consequently very lonely people. She was a gentle child of nature who talked to her birds as they came to be fed by her every day, and she seemed to hear the voices of growing things. The ordinary things of every day mattered very little to her. When her husband's guests came to stay she would make a special effort and would meet them for a short time every day. I felt so sorry for her; she seemed to me so utterly forlorn. Her husband had to go away constantly, looking after his railways, and she would be left with her birds and the trees and flowers for company. She had one great friend, Mrs Ricketts, the wife of one of his chief engineers, who lived further up the line at Shan-Hai-Kuan. She understood and really cared for her, but she seldom saw her. When, later on, I came to know Mrs Ricketts well, she and her husband became our greatest friends in China. She was a North Irish woman of great charm, married to a delightful Englishman, and she belonged to an old Irish family. Everyone knew her in that part of China, for she and her husband kept open house and anyone visiting Shan-Hai-Kuan was always welcome.

On Vernon's return to Tientsin, Miss Henry and I came back to the rather gay life there, meeting many people who had come out from Europe to see the condition of affairs in China. We saw much of my cousin Tommy Scott, later General Sir Edwin Thomas Scott, who was a most amusing raconteur and could keep us all in fits of laughter without stirring a muscle of his most expressive face. We missed him greatly when he had to go home.

Things were beginning to settle down quite peacefully in Tientsin when we heard of a tragic accident that occurred at the Chinese Winter Palace in Peking where fire had broken out and the German General Schwarzkopf was killed. Was it by accident or design that this fire had started? Who could tell? There seemed a fatal streak running through the German High Command for it was not long before another General was burnt to death in his special asbestos-lined railway car. His stove had been kept well stoked, for the weather was bitter cold. It was presumed that something had knocked over the stove and before the General could be rescued the car became like a furnace, no one could approach it and he met a terrible death. General Waldersee was now without his two most able commanders and felt their loss desperately. In the fire in the Winter Palace he had lost most of his own personal possessions, everyone sympathised deeply with him for he was very well liked. His was not an easy task, for to be a Commander-in-Chief of all the various troops required great tact and understanding.

Vernon was making new friends amongst civilians and military people. There were many places of interest to visit now that the times were more peaceful. I was asked to go and look round the native city in Tientsin, though it was still too soon to go there without protection. We made up a party and Colonel Hamilton Bower sent an escort of soldiers from the Chinese regiment he had at Wei-Hai-Wei, and as these men were absolutely loyal to the British we could be sure of a successful tour of the town. Starting off early one morning we attracted much attention with our procession of rickshaws. Our ride was full of perils, from the deep potholes and uneven ruts in the bad roads, for our coolies could scarcely keep the rickshaws from turning over and flinging us into the slimy mud. We visited what was known as the thieves' bazaar, where bargains were to be picked up, but I saw nothing much I wanted to buy. The shops themselves I much admired with their very ornate balconies and delightful china tubs to sit on, some of them most valuable old china. Then the tall ornamental shop signs fascinated me, many of them on long poles, generally very bright and painted red with black or gold ornamentation. The Yamens, the official residences of the Chinese magistrates, were very impressive and dignified, their many courtyards surrounded by the dwelling houses and entered through highly ornamented doors. The courtyards themselves were gay with flowering plants in brightly coloured pots and most picturesque. Returning through the narrow streets we met a large funeral procession, and waited to let it pass. We watched the many gaudy carriages and cars which carried an effigy, all the requirements of the man whose body was in the coffin, and which he would surely need in the new life – there was the house, horses, servants, food, everything possible that he could want and all were burnt later on to make sure that he got them! Most of the mourners, dressed in white, rode in horse-drawn carriages, the official carriages quite impressive with their large gold knobs in the centre of the roof. As soon as the procession had passed we drove on home as quickly as the bad roads would allow.

The following day Vernon and I got early to the station to catch the train for Tangshan. We had gladly accepted an invitation to stay with Mrs Kinder again. We were looking forward to getting away for a few days from Tientsin where it was now very hot and stuffy, and when we reached Tangshan there was a breeze blowing which was very refreshing. The Kinders' garden was shady and delightful to sit in and the house very cool. We were taken for a visit to the coalmines and Mr Kinder took us down himself, accompanied by the head mine officials, who were very proud of the efficiency with which the mines were run. We were struck with the evident well-being of the miners and the goodwill evident everywhere – the people in the villages and in the towns looked very flourishing, for the workers were well paid and were contented. They themselves had protected the mines and railway workshops from the fury of the Boxers during the war, and had kept Tangshan quite undamaged. Mr Kinder drove us over to see the summer residence belonging to Li Hung Chang, the famous statesman of the days of the ascendency in Peking of the Empress Dowager. When he wanted a rest, Li Hung Chang could go and enjoy a quiet time in his delightful house at Hsukochuang, where slender trees grew tall and leafy in the gardens; most unusual, for the trees that we always saw were stunted and short, indeed they were never given the chance to grow. The Chinese hunger for anything that would burn in their charcoal stoves and keep them warm in winter urged them to cut anything in the way of a tree that they could find. No bush or tree could grow unless protected, and this was done near the temples or on private property. The little stunted fir trees on the private burying places always attracted attention, in that very treeless part of China.

On another day we climbed up the hills to see two 'joss houses' or temples, and were not very much impressed by them for the Gods in tawdry flaring colours are not imposing, though the placid, meditating face of the big central Buddha gave us a feeling of beauty and restfulness. In front of this figure the candles and lamps were lit at night and joss sticks burnt when prayers were offered, and a quaint old temple bell rang every night at about ten o'clock to remind the faithful to pray.

Our visit was all too short, for Vernon was recalled from leave and told to keep himself in readiness to travel into Manchuria for about a month. This was rather depressing news I thought, for I had not yet got used to my new surroundings, and still disliked living alone with only Chinese servants to look after me. Those who had lived in China for many years really trusted and loved the cultured Chinese: the honest merchants, and the clerks and servants who served them, they knew well who were the thugs and the bad people who had been worked up to start the Boxer War. But I was still too much of a greenhorn to understand how to differentiate, though later on I began to see for myself what a fine people the Chinese really are.

9

RAILWAY STAFF OFFICER AT SHAN-HAI-KUAN

❧

V ernon found that his knowledge of the Russian language was most useful, for there were many conferences to attend where the generals commanding the various forces required interpreters. The Chinese railways were being administered partly by the British, and the northern section by the Russians, the junction of the two administrations being at Shan-Hai-Kuan. From there the Russian section continued towards Newchuang and eventually came within easy reach of their own railway in Siberia. From Shan-Hai-Kuan to Tientsin was the British section, another from there to Peking, and a further section from Tientsin to the port of Taku. At Shan-Hai-Kuan the British and Russians had each their own railway staff officer managing their districts through the local Chinese stationmaster. This man was most wise and tactful, full of the quiet patience of the Chinese and extremely intelligent. As the month of May ended the heat was pretty great, it boiled up even more in June and July, and Vernon and I, not being used to it, felt it considerably. He often had a sort of dysentery, which we found was the result of the hardships and insanitary conditions he went through during the siege. His meals of fly-infested food were the chief cause.

We met a new friend that summer, a Mrs Robertson, who had recently married our local doctor. She lived in a lovely house that had a large cool garden with shady trees, and often asked us in to enjoy it for we had no garden at all. Our house stood beside a bare compound given over to the servants' quarters, and it was a welcome relief for us to find somewhere to be cool in the evenings.

On Sunday June 23rd we went to a Thanksgiving Service for the Relief of Tientsin and this was followed by a big official lunch in honour of all the relieving forces. It was a very festive occasion: excellent food, many speeches, and an exceedingly good German military band played some well-chosen classical music and charmed all the guests, for our local musical efforts were very limited.

Shortly after this Vernon got his orders to take up the duties of railway staff officer at Shan-Hai-Kuan and to leave almost at once. Now our plans had to be completely changed. Fortunately, we could give up our house quite easily, as it was only lent to us by a friend who was ready to return to it whenever we wished to leave. Vernon went off to prospect and see what accommodation could be got for us, and met Mr and Mrs Ricketts, the delightful couple who lived in a most English-looking house near the railway. Mr Ricketts ran the section of the railway that was temporarily under the military orders of the British Railway Administration. Vernon found Mr Ricketts most anxious to do all he could to find us somewhere to live, but so far he could see no prospect of anything except to stay in a sleeping car at the railway siding. Vernon's office was just two rooms at the station, kept for the English side of the station, the other side being occupied by the Russian railway staff officer. As Vernon stood on the platform he could look out onto the Manchurian border and there, as far as the eye could reach, he could see the Great Wall of China, this amazing structure built to follow the border, up and down the hills and mountains, over precipitous cliffs and along the valleys, indeed a wonderful feat of engineering. It is constructed of great bricks nearly two feet long, and six or eight inches in depth and breadth, immensely stronger than anything we could produce in brick, for these had lasted for many centuries. It was intended as a fortification to exclude the Manchus from China proper, and was intersected near the towns with wonderful gates of the most picturesque architecture. The Wall itself ended in the sea on the coast not far from Shan-Hai-Kuan.

Vernon was very much intrigued by all the various people he had to deal with at Shan-Hai-Kuan station. First there was the Chinese stationmaster, whom he really liked, for he was most upright and dealt so wisely with the complicated situations of a station and railway run by both British and Russian officers. Presented then was Captain Ignatieff, the Russian railway staff officer himself. He was a curious, friendly sort of person, quick to take offence, rather self-important, possessed of none of the charm of the Russian officers we had met who came from St Petersburg under the Tsarist court influence. These latter were courtly, highly cultured, exceedingly wary and most pleasant to deal with, but there were none of this type of officer in Shan-Hai-Kuan, where several Siberian regiments were stationed. Then there was Mr Ricketts, the charming and delightful Englishman who was really master there, but now had to work with the two military staffs on the station. It was a very interesting situation for Vernon, and gave him a chance to use his diplomatic gifts. He was determined to keep on the good side of Captain Ignatieff and then steer clear of obstacles with all the others. Mrs Ricketts asked him to stay with them till he could find some place to sleep in, and after a time the station rooms used for an office became his sleeping quarters. For me it was another matter, where could I go? At first the sleeping car parked in the siding had to do; it was most uncomfortable, as the hard seats used as bunks were like our benches in the park and no amount of blankets could make them anything else but utterly, relentlessly hard. A hole for one's hip would have made all the difference.

It was exceedingly hot and I longed for a decent bath and I got one, for Mrs Ricketts offered to let me use her lovely bathroom and it was luxury after the small tin tub I had been using! Mr Ricketts now wondered whether he could turn one of the rooms in Vernon's office into a bedroom for me, as he had some spare furniture, made in his workshops, which he could put into it. This would be temporary he thought and would do till he could think out some way of turning one of his large, solidly constructed stores and tool sheds into a dwelling house. He found that with many alterations and large windows he could give us one that would provide four rooms for us: a large bedroom and another little one, a small sitting room and a tiny drawing room. There was a yard leading off from it, and another shed which could be turned into a couple of rooms to provide kitchen and coolie quarters. I never discovered what alternative accommodation Mr Ricketts found to house his tools and stores. Our house became known as the 'domtchick', Russian for 'small house', and just stood a few feet away from the points and intersecting rails where the locomotives came up to switch on to another line. The Russians, according to their rules, ordered that all locomotives must whistle on approaching this intersection, again whistle long and loud when they were actually on the points and loudly before leaving the points. This happened particularly at midnight, at four in the morning, and midmorning; pretty tough later on when our baby came and was housed in the room just near those wretched points. However, that realisation came later. Vernon and I for the moment were lodged in the office rooms of the station and Mrs Ricketts was giving us meals. It was wonderful to receive such hospitality, and nothing ever seemed too much trouble.

The first night in the station waiting room I slept badly and was attacked by fleas, which caused large red hives on my skin and were most irritating, but I had to make the best of it, I thought. Next morning I was just going to breakfast when I noticed patches on my dress as large as a half-crown of dark glossy masses. I stared incredulously and rushed to Vernon's office and asked him to look. He smiled but saw nothing particular, except large dirty blotches. 'They are moving,' I said with horror, and rushed outside to see how I could deal with these hundreds and hundreds of fleas in patches on my dress. I hurried to Mrs Ricketts, who had to put up with the invasion I brought with me. Quite unperturbed, she laughed heartily, saying I could certainly not sleep in that waiting room till it had been cleared of those fleas! Vernon had been there day after day and never felt any inconvenience; but as for me, well, that was a different matter, they fairly hopped towards me! Well, what was to be done now? I had a bright idea and asked the doctor attending the native hospital how he kept down fleas, bugs, etc. Quite easy, he said: 'First put out the floor matting in the grilling midday sun, for no insect life can live through it, then sweep over the matting every day with tea leaves soaked in carbolic and you will be alright.' I had this done and I saw no more fleas and was now able to go back to the waiting room and sleep in peace, except for the early morning mob of loud-voiced Chinese who bought their railway tickets at a tiny window of the office next door to my waiting room. We were certainly having plenty of experiences. When we lived at Shan-Hai-Kuan, crowded as it was with troops of many nationalities, the Ricketts' house was always full, they entertained the most cosmopolitan crowd, and all were made welcome, for their house had become the centre of attraction.

Many fortifications lined the coast near Shan-Hai-Kuan and were now occupied by troops of the various nationalities that had been sent to the rescue of their legations and to save their nationals trading in China. The Italians were in one, the French in another, a most picturesque fortification where the commander brought his family and thoroughly enjoyed living there. The Russians were quartered quite comfortably, accompanied by many of their families, in a similar fort, and the Germans had one overlooking a very pleasant part of the coast, but they kept rather to themselves. The Americans came and went almost before we could get to know them and the Japanese occupied one of the largest forts in the vicinity. Few of the Japanese were able to speak anything but their own language and we could therefore not converse with them or get to know them, though any that were able to speak English were always welcome as our guests. Then there were the Indian Army contingents, from some of the smartest units, calvary regiments, and part of a Ghurka regiment. There was certainly plenty of variety in the daily life of those who had to work together under such unusual circumstances.

Vernon thoroughly enjoyed dealing with so many different people of unfamiliar mentality whose approach to solving the problems that so frequently presented themselves was often so strange. He advised me now to go off to Tientsin where I had arranged to go to a hospital for the birth of the baby. He was storing up his leave to come and visit as soon as possible. The doctor in Tientsin whom we knew and liked had asked me to stay at his house for a short time, and his wife made me very welcome when I arrived. Her lovely shady garden was so delightful for the heat was still pretty unbearable. I wondered where I should go when my visit was over, for I had just been informed that the hospital I intended to go to would not take me. Vernon and I could not afford the enormous prices charged in the only hotel, for we had but little money to spare when all our ordinary expenses were met, and things looked pretty grim. It seemed too good to be true when a woman I had never seen before walked in one morning and said that she had heard of my plight and wondered whether I would come to her house, a large one, for she would be only too delighted to have me. I could hardly credit such generosity from anyone, let alone from someone I had never met before, but such is the hospitality and kindness you meet when people are very far away from home and they have difficulties and dangers to face in common. There is a camaraderie that is only met under the circumstances that we were all living in.

I asked my doctor what he thought, for I felt most diffident about imposing myself on a perfect stranger, but he, of course, jumped at it; it saved him from a dilemma, for he could think of nowhere for me to go. I very gratefully accepted this invitation and after the baby was born and a good many trials had been faced quite successfully I managed to arrange to go back to Shan-Hai-Kuan and live in the tiny house now quite ready for us to live in. A nice woman came to me as amah and we began to settle down. It was now October which had set in much cooler than usual and the weather was really lovely, and the fact that Vernon had no asthma to bother him made work a pleasure and he was thoroughly enjoying life. He had to make much use of the languages he knew in dealing with the officials of the various army contingents stationed near Shan-Hai-Kuan, also a ready wit was required in working with the Chinese element. But most important of all he made a success of keeping on the good side of his opposite number running the station staff of the Russian controlled portion of the line which ran into Manchuria, and Captain Ignatieff became a really good friend.

The 30th Punjab regiment had now taken the place of the Ghurka regiment which had returned to India. The Ghurkas were very popular with the Chinese; their smiling, courteous behaviour and their courageous bearing in all circumstances had made them much respected, contrasting very favourably with the rather overbearing attitude of many of the other troops in occupation there. We had now quite a pleasant little English coterie, and later on acquaintance with Russian artillery officers' wives and their families and with the wife of the French Colonel commanding the fort occupied by French troops enlarged our circle. Life became quite gay and we lived happily in this up-country life.

10

WE MAKE FRIENDS

❧

Vernon had to be on the station platform always at midnight and again at four in the morning. He found it quite easy to be there on time, for the baby preferred to be awake at night, often very noisily, and his amah let him do exactly as he pleased! As the winter came in with the dry, intensely cold winds of North China we had to resort to using 'army issue' stoves; these made of iron, with flues running up the walls and out into the open, had the effect of drying up the air so much that we felt like a chip and longed for some dampness to penetrate through our paper-covered windows which emitted no air whatever, not even through the small panes of glass let into the centre, which we could not open. Fortunately the tiny dining and drawing rooms had small glazed windows through which we could look out, but what air we got had to be let in through opening the hall door. Poor old amah could not make out why I kept on poking my fingers through the paper windows just to enable us to breathe more comfortably – all she thought of was to keep out the cold.

Our first experience of a really cold Chinese winter was an eye opener. When snow came, it was just like fine powder: no moisture in it, the wind cut through you like a knife, dust storms were unbearably cold and brought clouds of sand with them, yet there was also brilliant sunshine at times and wonderful skating on the ponds nearby. The river creeks, frozen thick, brought us opportunities of being driven along in tiny sledges known as 'peidses'; they were propelled by a pole with a strong metal point on the end, and pushed by coolies whose steering was as quick as it was sure. It was delightful speeding along these ice-bound creeks, almost like sailing, and most exhilarating in the crisp cold air. I was no skater but Vernon was good, and he got plenty of fun for there were many gay parties on the ice. The Russians skated beautifully, one in particular, Madame Tretiakov, who was a most skilful performer. She was also a superb dancer, but she was the oddest person. On one occasion she asked us out to visit her in the fort where the Russians were quartered, and when we got there she seemed almost too ill to move. She always felt ill, she said, but when the conversation interested her sufficiently she would forget all about it. If somebody played the piano she would dance round in the wildest way and ask for more and quicker music. One night, some of the Russian contingent asked us out to see the sports they had organised for their troops, by torchlight. It was a very dark night, and a wild and wonderful sight met our eyes as we stepped out onto the arena formed by a semicircle of mounted Cossack soldiers, each man holding a long flaming torch blowing in the fitful breeze and shedding a weird strange light all around. Their long-tailed, long-maned ponies pawed the ground impatiently and a crowd of onlooking soldiers with their wives and families awaited the signal to begin the trick-riding events we had been invited to watch. As soon as we approached with the commandant the contest started, pair after pair of most skilful riders cantered past us giving wild and piercing shrieks as they speared the pegs, or lifted the handkerchiefs off the ground, most difficult to see in that flickering light. At the conclusion of the riding events dancing began and then our delicate little hostess came outside and joined the dancers. She stood, with the torches throwing dark shadows on the ground and watched the soldiers dancing frantically with swift jumps and twists, carrying out the well-known crouching movements with heels kicking out in the speedy rhythm of the national tunes. Then suddenly Madame Tretiakov tore into the middle of the ring and danced like she was possessed. She twisted and twirled at the most amazing speed, she swung round and round, and we, having seen her only a few moments before languidly lying on her sofa complaining of her aches and pains, were absolutely staggered. I shall never forget that night; it was so utterly unlike anything we had ever seen before, so typically Russian. Then the complete self-forgetfulness of the sick woman drawn by the irresistible rhythm of the national dances, and able to join in with a frenzy that left her eventually completely exhausted.

Vernon could talk Russian so well that he found it easy to enter into the thoughts and outlook of these rather uncouth Siberian Russians, for they were kindly people. Most of us could do no more than converse a little in French with those who could understand it, and we made contact as best we could. We were rewarded by a friendship not often given to foreigners. At first we had found them inclined to keep very much to themselves, but having once taken to us they remained our very good friends and trusted us. I think in truth that it was the atmosphere of friendliness radiating from Caroline Ricketts' house, always hospitable, always interested, which made all the difference to the outlook of all the varied elements that made up the community. We found we could really understand the differing points of view. If ever the League of Nations worked, it did so in miniature, at Shan-Hai-Kuan. After a couple of years we even got together an international club for friendly dances, dinner and sports and it worked well, giving us the gayest entertainment, where we could all be just as lighthearted as we wished. A wonderful flag designed to blend the flags of six nations flew from the club flagpole. Vernon got one of these flags and had it framed and I have kept it ever since as a memento of a very interesting experiment in friendship.

In the spring we left our little house, the 'domtchick', rather regretfully really, though thankful to get roomier quarters and a garden where we could grow our own vegetables. This new house belonged to one of the railway officials, who was away on long leave, and we could stay for several months. While we were there we witnessed one of the most comical incidents that occurred while Vernon was stationed at Shan-Hai-Kuan. One morning, looking out of the window I saw Vernon watching something that seemed to interest him as he stood on the railway platform. Suddenly I heard shouts and frantic hooting from a Russian locomotive that was blowing out clouds of smoke and travelling at pretty good speed. The stokers were shovelling coal onto the furnace with feverish zeal and looking up the line with most apprehensive faces. To my amazement, I suddenly realised that another locomotive was steadily approaching it on identically the same railway line. The scared stokers awaited the inevitable crash. It came with a loud bang, but a bad collision was averted by the fact that the drunken driver of the oncoming engine had sobered up sufficiently to put his brakes on, for he had overcome his indignation at seeing anything trespassing on what he considered was his own line. There was a considerable mix-up, also his locomotive had gone miles past his intended stop. All this was greeted with roars of laughter from both the English and the Chinese railway staff – Vernon watching from the platform was trying to keep a straight face for he saw the furious indignation of Captain Ignatieff, the Russian staff officer, who was striding off to order the arrest of the now very crestfallen drunken driver.

At 4am the next morning the Captain was still in a very bad temper. He was meeting the first train as usual at 4am and on this occasion his greetings were very cool indeed, but it was not long before the whole incident was forgotten and Captain Ignatieff's good humour returned. Those early mornings in winter and early spring when Vernon had to meet the trains tired him quite a bit, for he had bouts of asthma owing to the cold, however they did not affect his cheerfulness and he made very light of it.

As the warmer weather came in again we were plagued with mosquitos, so our friend Mr Ricketts ordered one of his workshop carpenters to put mosquito netting all along the verandah in the front of our house. The netting was strengthened with thin supporting cross pieces of wood, making the house look like a large meat safe. This now became its name, but we laughed at the jokes made at our expense, for we could sit in comfort, while our friends no doubt wished their houses had the same protection. I was always apprehensive of the hot weather since Vernon had suffered from the North China form of dysentery, so prevalent in Tientsin after the siege. There was a certain Dr Moorhead resident in Tongshan, who was famed for his researches in this disease and others prevalent in the Far East. We could always call on him if we thought any of us had a touch of this dysentery, but it meant a visit to Tongshan and having to stay there for a few days. Then our Japanese friend Mrs Kinder would invite us to her house with her usual kindly hospitality, and Dr Moorhead would come along and soon put our minds to rest. He took Vernon in hand so well that he eventually cured him.

11

A DISTINGUISHED VISITOR

❖

When the railway official who owned our little 'meat safe' house returned from leave, we had of course to find other accommodation and, once more, Mr Ricketts solved our difficulty. We moved into a really lovely house, which had been the residence of a local Chinese official, and were now very comfortable, for it had many big rooms and we could turn one of these into a study for Vernon. The house with its large devil screen was built with the usual two courts; the front one contained all the big rooms, their decorative windows looking out onto the courtyard. Each window had a small central pane of glass surrounded by beautifully carved tracery of woodwork, backed by oiled paper that made the rooms warm in winter and cool in summer. The devil screen was a most picturesque structure, like a short roofed wall long enough to extend well beyond both sides of the main doorway, and about four or five feet away from it. Spread across it was a really beautifully coloured and most decorative dragon, and this structure was intended to keep all devils from entering the house. Devils, you see, can only fly absolutely straight ahead and cannot deviate to left or right, therefore all doors in these houses were built exactly opposite each other, so that if by any evil chance a devil was to be able to get inside it would have to fly straight away out again. In spite of this protection we were not to utter one word of praise of the baby in the house. Vernon was warned never to say anything but that the child was a wretchedly poor specimen, ugly and not much use to anyone, then the devils would be satisfied and would not harm the miserable little boy. Sounds a pretty joyless creed, and the poor people of China had all this horrible philosophy drummed into them from earliest childhood; it applied to all good things that life can give. It was surprising how they managed to be so happy and contented, and marvellously unemotional on most occasions. Many, of course, were fatalists, and a good many were Buddhists; the latter did not believe in devils but Taoists all did.[1] In the ninth century the great philosopher Tao had taught his followers a religion of much purity and depth of thought.[2] It gradually became debased and produced this hideous fear of devils, corrupting the purity and truth of the philosophy that had been so evident in its early years.

Vernon could now really tackle the formidable task of learning to read and write the Chinese language in his spare time. It is largely a matter of memory, and quickness of eye to be able to master the meaning of the characters, each one denoting a word and each one monosyllabic – essentially a task requiring great patience and perseverance. The finest paintbrush is used to form the characters. It almost requires an artist to write out a letter or document, but 'foreigners', such as Vernon, used pencils or pens and did the best they could with them. Vernon had a very quick eye and could read the characters in a dictionary very swiftly. I marvelled at it, for I found it quite impossible to recognise each tiny stroke in a character as he did. He got hold of quite a good teacher who was really rather astonished at the ease with which he could pronounce the different intonations of the same-sounding word, for there are about four different tones for each word, each tone giving a different meaning. Such as 'hao', meaning good when pronounced very shortly, but if said with a drawl meaning something quite different, and so on. One woman laughingly told me she had asked her head boy for an umbrella, and she saw him labouring with the assistance of a coolie, to bring her a heavy piece of furniture, she having used the wrong tone in pronouncing the word. Well, this was a bit of an exaggeration, but certainly illustrated the difficulties of Chinese tones. Vernon aimed at learning at least a thousand characters, for without that limited amount he could hardly get along with his reading nor hope to pass the interpreter's exam, which he had originally come for. He was now only studying Mandarin Chinese writing and a sort of shorthand in use for ordinary business documents. He had not attempted to master any of the various other characters of Confucian or classical writings which were quite different. But he meant to get a good working knowledge of those in common use, and seemed to get through it amazingly well.

On Sundays Vernon had managed to organise a little church service and held it in the waiting room at the station. He got hold of a small harmonium, which Caroline Ricketts played; he himself read the service and our little English community sang the hymns most lustily. There was an English battery of 'pom-pom' gunners stationed not far away, and the men came to the service very willingly. Sometimes, on very rare occasions, a clergyman would come and take the service, for our bishop in Peking heard of our efforts and helped us whenever he could. Eventually the Society for Propagation of the Gospel, the oldest of our missionary societies, proposed building us a little church.[3] We received this news very gladly; they provided the funds, and then a tiny little red brick church was built close to the Ricketts' garden. We had our consecration service when a clergyman came from Peking. The little church was very simply furnished, and our harmonium sounded quite well with the small congregation singing to its accompaniment. I played it now, and was also chief choir, finding it quite strenuous to pedal hard and sing at the same time. Officers from the Indian regiments stationed at Shan-Hai-Kuan, and their wives, though only a very few of them had so far ventured out to China, formed part of our congregation. Also there were the Ricketts, their two children and their aunt, Miss Humphreys, each one counted very specially and their absence would be noted with concern. Eventually we had the first wedding service in our little church, also a christening and, sad to say, a funeral service. In so small a community a tragedy meant something that touched us all very deeply, and when one of our young army doctors met with a fatal accident it clouded our lives for a long time.

Vernon's work on the station frequently brought him into contact with very interesting people passing through or coming to spend a day or two at the various forts in the neighbourhood. On one occasion he let me know that he was bringing in a very distinguished guest, General Marchand of Fashoda fame, who had once, long ago, cut across our British interests in Africa, causing a good deal of unpleasantness between the French and ourselves.[4] By the time we met the general he had become very friendly to the British and we found him quite charming as he sat in our funny little dining room being waited on by our solemn-faced 'head boy'. General Marchand impressed Vernon greatly with his very distinguished bearing, his courtesy and thoughtfulness in conversing with him, a young English officer, for somehow he seemed to understand the circumstances in which we were then living. Vernon encouraged him to speak his mind and soon we realised that to him all that mattered was the honour of France, his beloved France, and his point of view was most enlightening on the subjects that affected us in the international situation of the day. Another most interesting visitor to Shan-Hai-Kuan was the famous old Chinese statesman Li Hung-Chang. Though he could no longer influence the government in China in the able manner of former days he was still held in great respect by the officials of the various nations represented at Peking.[5] Vernon was much impressed by his dignity and suave authoritative bearing – it was rare to meet people like him, he seemed to belong to a past era in Chinese affairs. The station at Shan-Hai-Kuan gave kaleidoscopic pictures of so many people just passing through who were of special importance in the rather chaotic times we were living in.

Few trains passed through in the late afternoons and then Vernon could go off and play tennis on the Ricketts' court where he was always welcome. We owed so much to the Ricketts who were the sort of linchpin round which our little world revolved. Their dinner parties were famous and were invariably followed by the most uproarious sing-songs. We dished up the old favourite tunes time after time, nobody seemed to tire of them and any new songs from the current musical comedies in London were very popular; they seemed, somehow, to bring us closer to the joys of home.

12

SHAN-HAI-KUAN REVERTS TO CHINESE CONTROL

❖

The head of the Russian-controlled section of the railway on the Manchurian side, and which ran up to Newchuang, was Baron von der Ropp, who was an excellent example of the culture and graciousness of those Russians who belonged to the courtly circles in St Petersburg. His wife, also charming, was particularly interested in Vernon when she discovered that he suffered from asthma, for her husband had had to contend with it for many years and had much sharper attacks than Vernon, for he was very stout which made things no easier for him. They became great friends, for the baron really appreciated Vernon's work and was always ready to see his point of view; things went very smoothly whenever he visited Shan-Hai-Kuan. He was eventually instrumental in gaining recognition at the headquarters of Vernon's work and presented him with a large silver bowl and tray of very ornate, but very beautiful design, which were inscribed with words of thanks from the Russian railway staff.

By September 1902 it was decided to end the foreign administration of the railway, and a date was fixed for the official handing over to the Chinese authorities. Vernon felt quite sad at the thought of giving up what had become such an interesting job, also he knew that it meant the end of his official work and the return to his studies of the interpreter's exam.

The date chosen for this ceremonial event at Shan-Hai-Kuan was September 26th. In command of the British contingent in that area was Colonel Dobbie, cousin of General Dobbie of Malta fame, and he was to bring a guard of honour, men from the 30th Punjab infantry, who were much respected in the district. The Russian head of the military railway administration was also to bring a guard of honour in order to welcome the Viceroy of Mukden who was to bring a retinue suitably impressive to mark this great occasion.[1] When the day arrived the station staff officers, Vernon and Captain Ignatieff, awaited the Viceroy who came accompanied by his band of musicians. They carried trumpets of strange shapes and sizes, and weird pipes and drums, for he was evidently not to be outdone by the Russians who brought a band, or by the British who arrived with a small fife-and-drum band. A huge Chinese dragon flag had been spread across the central station building and with much dignified bowing the Viceroy was installed in front of this flag, and now the ceremony started. At a given signal the Russian national anthem was played slowly and impressively, and the Russian flag was hauled down. The playing of the English national anthem followed this, and the Union Jack was lowered. And now came the solemn moment: the Viceroy called upon the official in charge of the strange-looking band, and amidst the roaring of pipes and resounding trumpets, drums beating a hilarious tom tom, the Chinese flag was hoisted on the central flagstaff. The courteous and dignified Viceroy received the good wishes of the departing foreign officers and the ceremony was over. Then the photographers, mostly Japanese, came along and took most excellent photographs which became interesting mementos of a very historic occasion. The station was once more under Chinese control and the stationmaster, who had become a real friend of Vernon's, was in full charge.

It was with great regret that Vernon said goodbye to all the people who had worked so pleasantly with him, and to the job which he had so thoroughly enjoyed. From now on he would be living in Shan-Hai-Kuan, quietly studying Chinese, and there would be nothing to distract him; life would be rather dull by comparison, for he would miss dealing with his station duties which often required so much tact and diplomacy.

The Ricketts arranged that we should go on living in the same house we were then occupying, and Vernon had to communicate with the War Office to sanction a further period of language leave which had originally been given him for two years only. The permission to stay duly arrived, and Vernon got to work with the assistance of his excellent teacher. It was a bitter, cold winter and our house none too warm, but we got quite a bit of skating which helped to break the monotony of the constant language lessons. A very warm spring the following year heralded an intensely hot summer. It was easy enough for me to go off to the seaside and get cool there, but Vernon had to stay at home working, always working, with an anxious feeling that it was more than possible that he might not be able to memorise a sufficient number of those complicated characters to pass his exam which he was to take in a few months time. If he failed he would have to stay on and take it again, and that would upset all our plans. When the day came for him to go to Peking for the exam he got an invitation from the Italian minister for us both to stay at his legation which we gratefully accepted. As we travelled up in the train Vernon was still feeling exceedingly doubtful, and rather depressed, but we were looking forward to our visit and he was outwardly very gay. I put away the rather awful thought that we might have to stay yet another year in China unless he succeeded at the first effort, for now our plans were eagerly turning homewards.

We were warmly welcomed on our arrival at the Italian legation and the minister's wife took me out sightseeing while Vernon struggled with his complicated exam papers. He managed to get away part of one day and we all went together to the Forbidden City and saw the wonderful Temple of Heaven, roofed with tiles of a deep shining blue colour, cone-shaped and capped with an enormous gold ball at the centre. The walls of the various courts surrounding the Temple of Heaven were topped with highly glazed rounded and enormous tiles in imperial yellow or bright green, the tiles at the angles of the walls being finished off with circular or semi-circular tile ends emblazoned with the imperial emblem of the five-clawed dragon. As we stood on the steps of the imposing stairway, flanked by red-painted ornamental railings, which leads up to the central temple, the sun was shining brilliantly on the brightly coloured tiles. But we were filled with sadness at the desolation we saw around us, for the fighting had been heavy in the Forbidden City and in the temple, and the destruction of the beautiful things it contained was wantonly barbarous. The European troops quartered there for a time had deliberately smashed the exquisite blue porcelain libation bowls of various shapes and sizes, which were quite irreplaceable, a lost art to make porcelain of such weight and colour. In the Forbidden City they had also burnt for firewood, or just deliberately broken up, some of the rare and beautiful rosewood and blackwood furniture carved with emblematic and most intricate designs, each one a perfect specimen of the work of highly skilled craftsmen. The Chinese of the old cultured classes looked on this destruction with disgust and contempt for the Europeans that could perpetrate such vandalism, and when we saw it we felt ashamed that in the name of reprisal for the war waged against us we should have destroyed such priceless things. We turned away with rather heavy hearts and went back to the legation.

Another day we drove a rickshaw to see the Peitang Cathedral, which Vernon had visited when he first went to Peking. I was intensely interested to see what he had already described, for here in this cathedral the desperate siege had taken place which was an epic of bravery and endurance. Those monks and nuns and the hundreds of refugees they were sheltering must have thought it almost a miracle when they saw a Japanese officer suddenly walk in, and realised he was there to herald the approach of the relieving troops. What rejoicing there was in spite of the sickness and distress they were suffering. They had listened for so long to the constant firing and could never guess that now the forces that were besieging them were themselves being attacked and overwhelmed! It must have been wonderful to see their joy.

In the legations too the desperate fear of complete starvation had become ever more insistent; the attacks from the Chinese troops were fairly accurately directed, and the guns they had mounted quite close to the walls enclosing the legations made it almost impossible for anyone to leave the shelter of the buildings. Sir Claude Macdonald had managed to get a message through to the relieving forces to say that only fourteen days of very scanty rations was left and the situation was desperate. Ammunition was running very low though the legation guards were very sparing of it, only using it to prevent the attackers suddenly swarming over the walls. When the first contingents of the relieving troops pushed into Peking through the water gate, they were only just in time to save them. There was but little resistance, for the Chinese commanders realised that it would be futile to attack so large a force.

Rejoicing was great in all the legations for the strain had been almost unbearable, and on hearing that the imperial Chinese court had fled, they knew that once more the best elements among the ruling Chinese would get the upper hand. The iniquitous Empress Dowager insisted on taking her son, the Emperor, with her though he would have gladly stayed behind.[2] He might have been a wise ruler, had the old Empress not incessantly intrigued against him, seeing that he never got the chance to create a party of his own who would have helped him to come to power. She kept him a virtual prisoner and eventually forced him to take his own life. She was an utterly unscrupulous woman whose whole desire was to be absolute ruler of China and would allow nothing to interfere with her ambition. She regarded her son with utter contempt, for he was in favour of reform had he been able to get into power. The wise and thoughtful Chinese, who had never approved of the Boxer Rebellion and were glad that it failed in ousting all foreigners, were only too thankful to see the imperial court in flight as were most of the people, for they both feared and hated the Boxers.

13

PEKING

❧

T he streets of Peking, especially those seen from the surrounding wall of the city, were of great interest and beauty: very narrow, with rickshaws plying their trade along uneven flagstones skirting the roadsides. Some streets were flanked with deep dusty ditches that, after rain, became squelchy with black mud. These were most unpleasant to fall into, were the rickshaw coolie unlucky enough to slip in a wheel and turn over. This nearly happened to me, but my clever coolie righted my falling rickshaw just in time. The shops along these roads were most picturesque with highly ornamented balconies and open fronts which attracted customers who were trying to strike profitable bargains with very wary shopkeepers.

Just outside every shop stood a tall red pole high as the rooftops. From each one floated gay little painted signs cut out in metal or wood denoting the goods on sale, shaped as hats, coats, shoes, all sorts, making a little chorus of clanking noises as they waved in the breeze. From a distance and especially from the city wall these long poles, often topped with gold, looked most enchanting and, had the streets been cleaner, nothing would have been more attractive than Peking's shopping centres.

Vernon, showing me round, and walking along the wall, pointed out the beauty spots. We looked into the compounds where the big houses of the wealthy were set round the paved courtyards in which we could see stone-rimmed pools cool and sided by trees. Also large decorative

Constance, in what was probably her wedding dress, 1900.

Mr. V. G. W. Kell.   Miss C. R. Scott.

Mr. Vernon G. W. Kell to Miss C. R. Scott.

MUCH interest was taken in this marriage, solemnised at the Parish Church, Queenstown, on the 5th inst. The bride was Constance Rawdon, second surviving daughter of Mr. James W. Scott, of Westlands, Queenstown ; the bridegroom being Vernon George Waldegrave Kell (Lieutenant 1st South Stafford-shire Regiment), only son of Major Waldegrave Kell (late 1st South Staffordshire Regiment), of 42, Clarges Street, Mayfair. The ceremony was performed by the Rev. Canon Daunt (rector) and the Rev. Mr. Allen (curate), the service being fully choral. As the bride entered the church on her father's arm, the choir sang the hymn " How Welcome was the Call," and, after the blessing, " O Perfect Love." Miss Scott looked extremely well in her gown of rich white satin, the slashed skirt opening over an underskirt of chiffon, embroidered in a shamrock design, and the long, graceful tunic having an edging of soft satin daisies appliqué. The bodice was enhanced with Irish lace. She carried the bridegroom's gift—a bouquet of white orchids, lilies of the valley, and orange blossom—her ornaments being a diamond pendant (from the bridegroom), a diamond and ruby bracelet (the gift of her mother), and a pearl star (a present from her sisters). There were six bridesmaids— the Misses Ruth and Vera Scott (sisters of the bride), Miss Edith Rawdon (her cousin), Miss Kathleen Horne, and the Misses Phyllis and Doris Scott (little cousins of the bride). They appeared in dresses of hailstone spotted muslin over white glacé, profusely trimmed with Valenciennes lace, and having as relief daffodil yellow scarves of crêpe de chine. They wore black picture hats, and carried shower bouquets of daffodils and lilies of the valley. The little girls wore white hats and carried baskets of the same flowers. All wore gold curb bracelets with pendant hearts, the bridegroom's souvenirs of the occasion. Lieutenant H. F. Parkin (1st South Staffordshire Regiment) was the best man. The reception took place at Westlands, the residence of the bride's father, the happy couple leaving later on their honeymoon. Mrs. V. G. W. Kell travelled in a smart tailor-made gown carried out in biscuit-coloured cloth, her beaver-coloured toque being finished with palest blue feathers. The presents were numerous and valuable. The bridegroom gave a diamond pendant. Mrs. J. W. Scott, diamond and ruby half hoop bracelet. Mr. J. W. Scott, half hunter watch and cheque. The Misses Ruth and Vera Scott, pearl pendant. Major and Mrs. Kell, set of silver spoons, forks, and set of knives. Mr. R Kell, cheque. Officers of 1st Battalion South Staffordshire Regiment, silver salver. Lady Arnott and the Misses Arnott, Irish point lace fan. Canon, Mrs., and the Misses

Newspaper announcement of Vernon and Constance's marriage, 1900.

Constance, Vernon and Mrs Thomas at the Thomas's house
in Troy, NY, USA, 1900.

Japanese girls in traditional dress during Vernon and
Constance's brief visit to Japan, 1900.

'The one and only real staff, North China, 1901. From left to right:
Captain Lee, Sir Sidney Barton, Colonel Dorward, Vernon,
Admiral George Holmes Borrett and Colonel Menzies.

Mr and Mrs Bullard at their home in Shanghai with
Constance and Mrs Bower, 1900.

Tientsin station under the Russians, 1900.

American, Indian and British troops, Tientsin, 1900.

Vernon Kell.

Shan-Hai-Kuan, East Gate.

Vernon and Constance with son James (Jim) in China, 1901.

Vernon in later life.

Vernon, Constance and youngest son Johnny.
Possibly in South Africa, 1926.

china tubs standing about in plenty, in which grew lovely oleanders and flowering shrubs of all sorts – most attractive and full of colour.

We were most impressed by the legation gardens, they seemed luxuriantly green with their many trees and shrubs, and gay with gardenias and a profusion of pink oleanders. For us it was a delightful sight, our eyes had grown accustomed to seeing nothing but the bare brown landscape everywhere except up in the hills near Shan-Hai-Kuan. In the villages and small towns nothing green ever seemed to survive, no trees or bushes, for every scrap of wood was collected to make the charcoal used in the little cooking ovens in the houses and also to heat the stone beds which were built along one wall of the sleeping apartment. A thin pipe was cut into the foot of the bed and glowing charcoal was inserted into the open end of it, heating up the whole heavy stone platform which seemed to serve as sleeping quarters for the whole family. Padded quilts were laid over the stone to lie on, and a very scanty lot of coverings seemed to me to be quite inadequate to keep out the cold of the severe winters. The bolsters intrigued us most of all, for they were as hard as stones and there were no pillows. In the houses of the rich, along the tops of these beds were hung the most beautiful embroideries about twelve or fourteen feet long according to the length of the bed, and about three feet wide. These tapestries depicted perhaps the Eight Immortals, each figure faultlessly designed, or some classical legend carried out in exquisite colouring. The furniture was all elaborately carved, and heavily embroidered scrolls hung down the walls. There were also silk and vellum pictures, some most valuable, of classical quotations done in sepia writing, and painted with the finest brushes. Vernon and I wished we could have visited some of these houses and met the interesting and influential Chinamen who lived in them, but the times were still too unsettled for any friendships between us to be developed.

It was now the last day of Vernon's exam; he was to finish in the afternoon and my Italian hostess and I went out for a walk along the wall. I waited anxiously to see if Vernon would soon join us. He had been feeling very depressed that morning and sure he had not a chance of getting through and we thought it more than likely that we should be staying on at Shan-Hai-Kuan for at least a further six months. Rather distractedly I looked in the direction that I knew Vernon would be coming out to us, but no sign of him. Suddenly I saw a smiling figure rush up to the road on the wall, and there he was telling us with delight that he had passed! Now he could enjoy the short time that was still left to see more of Peking.

How different it must all look now, with its wide, clean streets, no litter anywhere, orderliness and modernity having done away with so much that was picturesque, and all in the name of good planning – the huge present-day building and offices, the large blocks of flats, must have completely altered the face of Peking. Do those who live there now ever sigh for the days when life was not planned and the lovers of art and culture could do as they pleased?

We said goodbye to our charming Italian host and hostess with much regret; they had been so good to us and spared no trouble to show us round. But now we had to hurry back to Shan-Hai-Kuan and prepare for our return journey to England. Our departure was rather depressing for the Ricketts family, as we had been so happy together in that little community and our circle of friends had become very dear to us. The Ricketts family had meant just everything to us, and we realised that when we left there would be very few people to keep up the little society we had formed.

Vernon and I were looking forward with delight at the thought of our journey back, for we were to travel across Siberia, Russia, Poland and Germany and so home to London. We would take seventeen days all told, and Vernon decided to make it longer by breaking our journey on reaching Moscow and stay there for a few days.

We had one amusing experience shared with the Ricketts before we left. The local Chinese magistrates gave a great banquet as a farewell to the departing officers of various nationalities and to the railway officials, our old friends the English engineers, who were now once more running the railways. This banquet was to be on an especially great scale, for a troupe of actors was engaged to produce a play as entertainment for the many guests. The wives of the officers and officials had been invited by the magistrate's wife to a separate meal in the women's quarters of his large house, and they were to be given the opportunity of seeing the play, though they were on no account to be seen by the host's own guests. Mrs Ricketts and her two boys, several officers' wives and I duly arrived at the women's apartments and were very courteously welcomed by our hostess and her friends and attendants. She led us into a dining room where a large table was spread out with dainty dishes, but covered, in deference to our European taste, with a rather crushed and dirty white tablecloth. Also she had provided us with some very rusty two-pronged forks and rustier knives, which she must have found most difficult to procure. As tablecloths were never used in Chinese households, where could she have found the rather frightful specimen she had managed to obtain for our table? The meal began with mutton cutlets, which were balanced in tiny bowls for us to cut with our rusty forks and knives! I noticed our hostess didn't try to master our supposed skill in dealing with so large a portion of meat sitting on such a small bowl, nor did any of her companions. We tried not to look dismayed as the cutlets kept on falling off the bowls onto the tablecloth. We looked enviously at the dainty food served to our hostess and her friends: small slices of fish and meat; vegetables delicately cut out in small patterns and suitably coloured; thinly cut, rose-shaped radishes; cucumber sliced so thin as to represent small leaves; turnips diced and flower-like, all looking so appetising that we sighed inwardly and presently gave up trying to cut up our impossible cutlets. Our hostess watched us and presently signed to her servants to hand us her own dishes. She was no doubt surprised at our discourtesy in setting aside what she had taken so much trouble to provide. As a special mark of respect she now took some of the food from her own bowls and gave choice pieces to her nearest neighbours, and we wondered what we might do to indicate our appreciation of her courtesy. When the meal ended, a box of cosmetics was passed round and we asked to be shown how to use them, all in dumb show, of course, for we could not speak a single word to each other. We put a lovely red colour on our cheeks, a small dab on our chins and a splash of colour on our foreheads, laughing gaily all the while for our Chinese friends had a plentiful sense of humour and there was now a really friendly atmosphere. Soon it was time to go outside into one of the courts, for we were to see the play staged in the banqueting hall where all our menfolk were being entertained. We were taken up into a sort of Punch and Judy structure from the upper part of which we could look into the hall and could remain unseen ourselves. A large bamboo blind screened us from view, and we could look through the slats and see everything well. To get to this curious observation post we had to climb up a clumsy stairway made of rounded wooden poles, most uneven and difficult to negotiate, and we watched with amazement the skill with which our hostess clambered up, for she had the traditional bound feet and hers were perfectly small. We had not been long gazing at the curiously garbed actors and listening to the cymbals, flutes, drums and horns giving out most discordant sounds, when the Ricketts' children suddenly managed to pull aside the tightly fitting bamboo screen – they had got tired of their limited view and were determined to see everything quite unhindered. Our hostess looking much concerned but also, I thought, rather pleased, drew back quickly for now the men feasting below could see her. I caught sight of Vernon who smiled up at us, as did many of our European friends, but the Chinese guests looked decorously the other way, and we realised that our hostess and her friends really dare not allow the children to embarrass them so much.

We longed for an interpreter to tell us what the play was all about, and explain the pageantry. It was quite evidently an ancient classic, judging by the costumes and by the posturing of the actors. We were really sorry when this entertainment ended and as we left and thanked our hostess we asked her to come to tea with us, which she accepted as soon as an interpreter, who had been summoned, could make our meaning clear.

When the magistrate's wife did eventually come to see us she brought her son, a boy of about nine years old, and her duenna with her. She arrived when our baby was asleep in his cot, which happened to be trimmed with white muslin over silk. He was asleep and the Chinese ladies looked into the cot with horrified faces for, as their mourning is white, and the cot was white, they gazed at this fair-skinned child and feared the worst. Just at that moment the baby turned and opened his big blue eyes to look at them with astonishment, at which the ladies turned to me with delight and admiration, for they had never seen a flaxen-haired boy before. We then went into our tiny dining room for tea and when the baby was brought in they expressed by every sign they could think of how pleased they were with him. After tea they went to inspect my bedroom and the duenna got onto my bed and rolled backwards and forwards on it saying, 'Hao, pu hao.' 'Good, very good.' I could just understand that. She was enchanted with the spring mattress and with the blankets and coverlets, all so new to her. Well, that tea party was an unqualified success, and my guests left well satisfied.

But we could not always find our experiences as pleasant as this one. We came close quarters with the fearful poverty and suffering of some of the people. One bitterly cold winter's day, when a cutting icy wind was driving with merciless fury into every crevice of our little house, Vernon and I decided to go for a walk in spite of the bitter cold. We had walked quite a long way when we heard a strange moaning sound and, looking round, saw crouching close to the ground a boy of about nine years old and wearing no clothes, but a wretched bit of sacking to protect him from that dreadful wind. The temperature was well below zero. We hurried off to try and find some shelter, but there was nowhere and the nearest was our own house. That was a long way off and on getting there we asked the house boy what could be done. But he took it all as quite ordinary, only our amah said: 'Oh Missy, that boy he makes die.' We asked the stationmaster, but he could think of nothing immediate, for the boy was too far away. Could he think of anything we could do to prevent such terrible things happening to helpless children, or did he know of anyone in the town who could bring charity to families so poor that they could not clothe nor shelter their children? He said there was a missionary who could perhaps advise us, and we hurriedly got into touch with him. We collected some money for him to dole out to the most deserving cases and when we gave it to him we thought he looked very doubtful. He returned after a week's trial, and said he was giving it up. He was so mauled and molested by little roughs who sprang upon him the moment they heard that some foreign ladies had offered to help them with money during the bitter weather, that it was as much as his life was worth to continue dispensing our small sums in charity. He found it impossible to reach the worst cases, and the less deserving ones were far too aggressive, so he begged to be excused! It was disappointing to realise that some utterly heartless and wicked parents might actually send out their children half clothed in the bitterest weather to make our hearts ache and so induce us to give them money. But that dying child left an awful impression, and we realised the relentless forces of ignorance and cruelty we were up against.

Another time, also in the winter, I was in the train going to see a friend for tea, many miles away, for we thought nothing of distances when we could make use of the railway. On looking out of the window as our train drew up at the station, I saw a beggar sitting on the ground. Beside him he had placed his two frozen feet! There they were for all to see – I suppose he had lost them owing to frostbite, and he had turned his misfortune to commercial use! I could not look at him, it was so horrible. At Shan-Hai-Kuan everything was decent and in order. The worst thing I ever saw there was the punishment of railway thieves who were generally dealt with summarily by having to wear a heavy square wooden board with a hole in the centre for the head to go through, and on it was inscribed the offences of the culprit. He had to stand or sit, wearing this heavy board for many hours at a stretch, till the punishment was considered sufficient for the offences committed. The thieves took it all quite philosophically, but found it irksome to be unable to reach their faces to flick off flies in summer or shield themselves from the wind and weather in the winter. As far as I could gather, the station was very well conducted, and there were few unpleasant incidents.

14

FAREWELL

❖

But to return to our farewell parties, one of them in particular is imprinted on my memory. The Ricketts had asked many friends to meet us at a big dinner, as a last social function, and as we were sitting together enjoying the final dessert course and wine was flowing freely, the head house boy brought in a telegram and handed it to Vernon. I caught my breath, for it was my constant dread that something would prevent us leaving for home, possibly a message from the War Office ordering his return to his regiment now stationed in India, or a postponement of some sort to cause us to alter our plans. I could see the official form and Vernon's look of surprise as he read the telegram, for indeed the order had come telling him to await instructions to take up another appointment. My heart sank, for I knew Vernon needed time at home to recuperate; he was tired and run down and I feared another hot summer might really make him ill. What were we to do? Our packing was nearly complete, our cases, all but our immediate baggage for the train journey through Siberia, were ready to be sent home by long sea, our plans were all made. It seemed a shattering blow, and I felt pretty miserable. Vernon laughed a little wryly as we left the dinner table and went into the drawing room. As usual I was asked to sing and entertain the guests, I made a move towards the piano rather reluctantly, when I suddenly caught sight of a mischievous twinkle in Caroline Ricketts' eyes, and realised that they had all been making fun of us and it was all a huge joke! They had got hold of an official form and stamp and prepared the whole thing very carefully. Everyone was in fits of laughter, and now we could join in and laugh at ourselves.

It was a very happy party after all, really the gayest of all our goodbyes. We should miss all the fun of our small social functions and especially the dances at our international club. I think we should certainly miss the friendly invitations of our Russian friends who always made us so very welcome. At Christmas time we had shared in their festivities and were greatly impressed by the beauty of their tall, well-shaped Christmas trees, decorated entirely in silver with hundreds of white candles and shimmering cascades of silver tinsel, no note of colour anywhere. It seemed strange that of all the nationalities we met at Shan-Hai-Kuan, the Russians had become most intimately friendly with us, and yet we had started by finding them more distant and difficult to deal with than any of the others.

Among the Germans we had one particularly interesting friend, Captain von Butler from Wurtemburg. He seemed almost like one of ourselves – he was so broadminded, thought like us, talked like us, he had a most unusually tolerant outlook, and his charm of manner made him most attractive. We found it no easy matter making friends with other Germans stationed there, for the fort they lived in was very far away and they seldom came in to Shan-Hai-Kuan itself. Most of our friends were among the British occupation troops, officers of the 30th Punjab infantry and their wives, and the REs temporarily in charge of the railway administration. Then there were the engineers who were on the railway and had been in China for years; we knew many of them. Those engineers were men of vision, pluck, and hard work, of whom we could be very proud. Their influence over the Chinese who came in touch with them was incalculably valuable, they were trusted and respected and, in return, they too gave respect and trust to the splendid Chinamen they had to deal with. As a friend of these British engineers, Vernon was accepted with special regard by the Chinese he worked with, and when we eventually departed from Shan-Hai-Kuan Vernon was given some lovely rolls of brocaded silk by the stationmaster as a parting present and token of respect. The day we left, the engine which was taking our train through to Neuchuang was hung round with fire crackers which were exploded as the train started so as to make sure there would be no devils to spoil our journey or frighten us in any way, a delicate attention that we realised was a special honour paid to Vernon.

Our amah insisted on travelling with us a day's journey as far as Neuchuang. We were really very fond of our Chinese servants, and they liked us too. We said goodbye to the Ricketts with very sad hearts, they and the children waved us off and we wondered when we should meet again. Pointz Ricketts travelled with us as far as Neuchuang in Manchuria and he came to see us safely through and to hand us over to his friend who was running the large section of the line, with Neuchuang as headquarters. He had a big house and asked all to stay the night and had invited many people to meet us at a dinner party he was giving in our honour. Lily Humphreys, Caroline Ricketts' sister, was travelling home with us, and she gave me a helping hand with our small son as soon as the amah left us. The next day we waited till evening to board a small steam launch which was to take us across the Gulf of Liautung to a small port where a loop line connected us with our train to Mukden which would then take us on to Harbin. There we should join the main Trans-Siberian Railway. It was on a very stormy night that we crossed the northern end of the Gulf, and our launch, plunging and tossing, shipped plenty of water as the waves broke over us. There was only a small shelter to keep us from being completely soaked and it was a very cold night. We were thankful to be landed at last and taken to the station where our train awaited us. Our accommodation seemed most inadequate after the comforts of our special car on the Shan-Hai-Kuan train. We were told much about the luxuries of the Trans-Siberian trains, their big roomy coaches gave passengers ample room to spread themselves and stow away the many pieces of hand luggage needed for so long a journey. The wide gauge of Russian railways certainly made it possible for the coaches to be extra comfortable. There was a wintry feeling in the air and we were glad to find the carriages well heated, almost too much so – we found it impossible to get a window opened. On one occasion, by dint of much cajoling, we persuaded the car attendant to open the window, much to the indignation of our fellow passengers in the other compartments. But we soon found out our mistake, for bits of glowing cinders from the engine, which burnt wood as fuel, were blown into our compartment and into our eyes, and we reluctantly acknowledged ourselves beaten over the question of fresh air. The only relief we could get was when we pulled up at a station, and could rush out and breathe really lovely exhilarating air of that bracing part of Siberia. Vernon speaking Russian so fluently could get all our wants attended to, and I was specially thrilled to find that he could order fresh milk to be delivered at various stations en route, for our use, otherwise there was nothing but tinned milk of the thickest and sweetest description. We could also get so-called fresh eggs. I say 'so-called' as they were mostly very stale, though not actually uneatable. The stations we passed through were very primitive-looking – just a small wooden station building, a short platform where Chinese coolies stood about to deal with luggage, should there be any. We changed into the main Trans-Siberian train at Harbin, a rather important-looking junction, and found our 'wagon lits' comparatively luxurious after the train we had left which boasted of little comfort. There was an excellent dining car serving well-cooked meals and very good attendants to look after us. We met some amusing passengers amongst whom were Russian officers delighted to meet an Englishman who could talk their language. We used to abandon small James to their tender mercies and they would push all the tables in the dining car to one side, and play all sorts of games with him on hands and knees keeping him amused by the hour during that long journey.[1] The countryside looked more and more wooded, especially after we had reached Manzhouli and then, as we neared Chita and the Yablonovy Mountains, the scenery reminded us a little of Switzerland. We saw very few Europeans at the stations, and the villages we passed were few and far between, each seemed to have a little church painted white, with its tower adorned with onion-shaped domes, some painted gold, some yellow, giving a lovely touch of colour against the dark background of the fir trees. There was snow on the ground and on the rooftops of the small houses, though it was so early in the autumn. It all looked so refreshing to our eyes accustomed to the sand-coloured scenery of the part of North China we lived in. We wished we could have stepped off the train and taken more photographs to remember it all by.

It seemed many days before we reached Lake Baikal where we were to leave the train and take a ship across the lake, for the tunnel skirting it, and being driven through very mountainous country, was still under construction. It was too early in the year for our ship, an icebreaker, to have her tanks filled with water to make her heavy enough to crash through the ice which would soon be thickly covering the lake, and she stood high out of the water which caused her to ride very lightly over the waves, rather like a cork bobbing about. The waters of that lake were something to remember, for the waves seemed to go every way; angry turbulent waves smashing about in a manner most devastating to those who were not the sturdiest of sailors, and even they looked a bit squeamish. The captain explained that there must be volcanic action below that lake, for the waves were so violent and the motion they caused unlike any other we had ever experienced at sea, but we found the captain's explanation cold comfort. Vernon was able to go in search of information as to what time we were likely to reach the other side of the lake, for there seemed to be no timetable to go by. Having gathered from some sailors what the arrival hour might possibly be, he came back to the saloon to find Lily Humphreys and me completely overcome, and everyone else equally sorry for themselves. We were a very miserable-looking little party as we disembarked, and to add to it all it was snowing and an icy blast blew fiercely into our faces as we trudged towards the station, where a primitive-looking train awaited us. The coaches were quite unheated, only hard wooden benches to sit on, for of course this train was only a link to take us to the junction not very far away, where we should once more find our 'train de luxe' awaiting us. We breathed a sigh of relief when we reached Irkutsk and got back into our comfortable coaches, where the dining car was so excellent and the attendants most obliging and friendly.

15

TRANS-SIBERIAN JOURNEY

❖

W e had by now made friends with several of the passengers, especially with the Russian officers travelling with us. One evening we were chatting gaily together when we noticed the train was swaying in a very odd way. We seemed to be clattering downhill at an ever-increasing speed and were going through a tunnel. I was a bit scared as the train began to lurch violently, and Vernon went off to question one of the railway officials. As we rocked more and more, and were travelling at alarming speed, I was not surprised to be told that the engine driver was exceedingly drunk! We were now rushing down a steep incline and the question was, could the train keep on the rails? The train officials and attendants looked very harassed, and then at last we felt the train slowing down which was fortunate as we were due to arrive at a station. Marvellous to relate, the train pulled up successfully and we heard with a sigh of relief that our drunken driver was being disposed of and another taken on instead.

As we neared European Russia, we passed through many miles of steppes: flat, dreary-looking country, rather like the Prairies in Canada, but not nearly so interesting, just miles and miles of dull country. The scenery gradually became beautiful again as we approached the Ural Mountains, and then, once more, we travelled through charming villages with their churches gay, with brightly painted domes, and groups of little houses. We halted at one station in the mountains where local metalwork trinkets were on sale. Some of these were very attractive and we bought one or two to remind us of our long journey through Siberia.

We were soon to reach European Russia and gradually the scene became much more familiar. We crossed the great Samara Bridge over the Volga, our long train moving slowly and cautiously over the centre portion. The bridge is immensely long, for the river is very wide and majestic. It was most exciting to feel that we should soon be in Moscow where we intended to stay for about a week. Vernon knew of a good hotel where we should not be very far away from the home of his old friend Madame von Kotsk. She would help us in finding some trustworthy person to look after small James when we went sightseeing. Vernon's knowledge of Russian made everything easy for us and also he knew Moscow well. It all turned out as he had hoped and now we could enjoy Moscow to the full. Together we went to the famous St Basil Cathedral, an amazing building, beautiful and yet strange with its intricate designs in stone both inside and out. The lovely paintings of the icons framed with priceless jewel adornments impressed me greatly, also the beauty of the metal work, and the ornate architecture, it was all so unlike our much more simple shrines of Christian worship. On leaving this very wonderful building we went to the Kremlin, a vast enclosure with crenelated walls forty feet high. Inside we walked through the staterooms of the palaces which even in those days contained glass cases in which were displayed the royal robes of bygone tsars, tsarinas and great nobles. We went on to look at the many churches and the lovely Cathedral of St Saviour. We only wished we had more time to spend reading up Russian history – the better to enjoy what we saw in the Kremlin. In the evening we were to hear the opera *Life for the Tsar* and the famous Chaliapin was to sing. We were thrilled, and as we walked into that historic opera house we expected a musical treat without equal. All that we saw and heard exceeded in beauty anything we had experienced previously in the world of opera, for this performance was superb. The singers, the chorus, the choreography were unsurpassed, Chaliapin was at the height of his fame, his voice carried us along with him as no other singer could have done, his acting intensely dramatic, the almost tenor quality of his bass voice so rare and beautiful, that we were left spellbound. We walked back to our hotel in silence, still living through those moments of exhilaration.

Next morning we found small James was not at all well, and this gave Vernon the opportunity to call in the doctor who had looked after him when he had been taken to the fever hospital where he had really first begun to speak Russian fluently. He came, very delighted to see Vernon and much interested to see his son who had just a slight upset, he said, and would be alright in a day or two. They talked of old times and when Vernon's old friend Madame von Kotsk also arrived they were a merry party, for she was so eager and vivacious, and her enthusiasm infectious. Looking back on that Moscow visit in later years, Vernon and I felt how fortunate we had been to have had the opportunity of seeing Moscow as it used to be, before all the sorrows and trouble had overwhelmed it and had changed the course of events in so large a part of the world. Very regretfully we left Moscow, our visit all too short, and started off once more in the train that was to take us to Warsaw and on to the Hook of Holland. Our long journey was nearly at an end; we should soon reach London and we did so in very good time, too good for those who hoped to be there to greet us at the station, for they were late and we felt a bit disappointed. However, just as we were wondering whether or not we should drive off to my father-in-law's house in Clarges Street, we saw my mother arriving and with her Vernon's father. So here we really were at last, it seemed like a dream to be back home again as we were hurried off to a hotel, for the Clarges Street house had been given up, and Vernon's people were waiting to go into their new home in Hertford Street. For the moment they were staying in the Curzon Hotel with my mother, and we were a very hilarious party.

16

HOME AGAIN

❖

After a few days' rest, Vernon reported at the War Office and was asked why he was not in India. Consternation on his part! The telegram telling him to rejoin his regiment in India had been sent to Shan-Hai-Kuan after we had left and were already well on our journey through Siberia. So the joke the Ricketts had played on us at their farewell dinner became reality! Vernon hastily came back to our hotel bringing the news that he must leave for India in about a month's time. I was staggered, for I felt that he must really get a bit of cool climate to set him up after what he had been through in North China. I begged him to try and get an exchange, which he did, for he found that one of his brother officers was only too glad to take his place in the battalion in India. Vernon went back to the War Office and informed those concerned of what he had been able to arrange and was then offered the sort of job he had hoped for. This started a career that, with various twists and turns, kept him at the War Office for the rest of his service and necessitated his living in or near London.

We sent James to my home in Ireland and took some rooms in Brompton Square which were pretty dismal, for our landlady gave out as little as possible but tried to get all she could out of us. My ideas of catering were somewhat hedged by the ease with which my Chinese cook had done all the house-keeping for me and kept a watchful eye on good value for money. But this English woman who wanted me to do all the buying of the food kept whatever she could of it herself and fairly snorted if I mildly suggested that the meats sent up to our table could reappear for another meal. Well, it simply wasn't good enough so we started house hunting. Vernon was now working as Staff Captain in the German section at the War Office. We thought it would be better to live just outside London where there was a good train service and as I had cousins living in Weybridge we went down to see them. The result was that we took a furnished house for a year to see how we liked Weybridge and to find out if the thirty-minute train journey to London would be sufficiently convenient for Vernon. It was a house in a small woodland area, and contained abominably hideous furniture, most difficult to live with, but the garden was nice. Vernon now started what we called his 'daily breading', joining the crowds of other daily breaders all bound for London in the morning and all processing back to Weybridge in the evening. It was all so utterly unlike what we were used to, Vernon away all day, and though his work in the German section was connected with intelligence work, it was at that time not particularly interesting. Our cousins in Weybridge, Walter Moresby and his wife, had a house quite close to ours, we saw much of them and a great friendship began between us.[1] I went back to Ireland to fetch James and his little Swiss girl nursemaid, and we got ourselves established in our house in the woods.

We had gradually got accustomed to our stubborn way of living by the time our second child Margaret arrived, but we disliked our house and hoped soon to find somewhere more congenial to live in.[2] Vernon was beginning to enjoy his work, which brought him in contact with many people of interest. General Sir Francis Davies, known as Frankie or Joe, who was then Assistant Director of Military Operations, was on the lookout for someone needed for an intelligence job.[3] He became interested in Vernon as he was a linguist and had experience in dealing with foreign officers on the staff and in various regimental positions, and he thought his qualifications might be useful.

At a much later date when the work of counter-espionage had begun to be really successful, Vernon would laughingly allude to General

Davies as the father of the work, for he had backed Vernon with much enthusiasm, using his influence to help him on. But the man who always claimed to have picked Vernon out for this intensely important job, which needed such careful and delicate handling, was Brigadier-General Sir James Edmonds, affectionately know as Archimedes, the famous sapper who later wrote that vast official history of the 1914–1918 war in many volumes, so penetrating in conception and in execution.[4] He became a great friend of ours in the years that followed. I remember on one occasion when he was speaking of counter-espionage, which had then proved itself and was known as MI5, that he said quietly to me, 'What was it that led me to pick out Vernon Kell for this job, which was so urgently needed for the safety of the country? How did I know that he was the best man to deal with it?' He smiled thoughtfully and looked penetratingly at me, evidently feeling that his inspiration had proved correct. I grew very confident of the success of Vernon's work as it gradually unfolded, though only those in touch with it could know, or indeed were permitted to know, of its extent and purpose. During the First War the prime minister, Mr Asquith, came to see the large map in the office and was shown the location of suspected spies.[5] He claimed, as he saw the extent of the work, 'why this amounts to a major victory,' so great had been this contribution to the successful countering of the enemy's intelligence organisation.

But I am digressing, and must return to the less eventful part of Vernon's career. His work in the War Office was all good practice for he met many men who were, later on, to be singled out for their outstanding ability and were to become famous. In Weybridge itself, Vernon soon made his mark as a man who gladly took an interest in whatever concerned the life of the village nearby, and in the district generally. There was talk of getting the local youth to learn how to shoot, with a view to increasing the size of our voluntary military organisations. The then Earl of Meath, a most delightful man who appreciated the possible dangers of a World War, tried to create enthusiasm for rifle-shooting training through the rifle clubs now being organised all over the country.[6] He was also most anxious to start an Empire Day campaign to make Queen Victoria's birthday, May 24th, an annual festival. He thought this would stimulate an interest in our achievements in the colonies and in the Empire. The rifle club idea spread in our village of Oatlands and members became most enthusiastic when their club was opened by Lord Meath. Vernon often spent the evening there and was good friends with the local young men and encouraged them to become good shots. He was now also getting to know the residents, especially those keen on games, and they arranged tennis and squash racquets for him often on Saturday afternoons, giving him a chance of plenty of exercise at the weekends. In connection with his War Office work, he was asked to be a guest at a dinner in London given in honour of Duke Tsai Tse who headed a Chinese military Mission and later was asked to take them to Aldershot and show them around, lunching at Woolwich where General French of 1914 fame entertained them.[7] Before leaving England they went to Sandhurst which they enjoyed and then Vernon saw them off to Paris, and an interesting episode came to an end.

Vernon, now in the German section, was constantly hearing discussions on the warnings that Lord Haldane was giving us on the work of the German general staff.[8] He had an unrivalled knowledge of the excellence and precision of their planning and he exhorted those in authority to stimulate efficiency if our general staff were to have any hope of success against this splendid fighting machine. Vernon had the greatest admiration for Lord Haldane who proved correct in all he had stressed and warned us about, when the war actually broke out.

Through the sections dealing with China and Japan, Vernon got the chance of once more meeting some of the men he had seen in Peking after the siege; men of much courage and excellence such as Sir Walter Hillier[9] and his blind brother[10] who were so entirely trusted and respected by the Chinese themselves. They were taking an interest in the newly formed China Society, which aimed at keeping together, both from a cultural and from a social aspect, these friends of China who had lived there and devoted most of their lives to what benefitted her as well as the trades or administrations they were working for. Vernon joined the society and found the lectures and entertainments both instructive and interesting.

He also became a member of the Royal Geographical Society and on one occasion heard the Duke of Abruzzi relate some of his experiences during his explorations, especially those in Africa, testifying to his great courage.[11] He made a profound impression on his audience.

It was very early in his career in the War Office that Vernon first met General Macdonogh, later General Sir George Macdonogh, who became a close personal friend.[12] He knew more about intelligence work than most and when, eventually, Vernon made special intelligence his life's work, he was always sure of good advice and strong backing from him. Vernon asked him now what he thought of his applying to go to the staff college, but he eventually decided that it would take too much time to complete the course.

We had now left our house in the woods at Weybridge and taken a much nicer one nearer the station and more convenient for Vernon. It had a long drive and quite a big garden kept up for us by the owner. She was a truly Victorian woman of the grand manner, and frequently brought in her guests to see us. She had let her house to us at a very moderate rental – all she wanted was to have congenial tenants as her neighbours, for her house and large grounds adjoined our garden. She became one of our best friends and a staunch admirer of Vernon's. Her daughter, the Marchioness of Bristol, often came in to see us; we found her a most interesting woman for there was something very unusual about her, as there certainly was also about her mother.

Early in the year 1907 my youngest sister married Captain Frederick Gilpin-Brown, a naval officer of great charm who was warmly welcomed in our family circle.[13] Vernon, meeting him for the first time at his wedding, hoped he might get an Admiralty appointment and give us a chance of getting to know him well. He was a man much beloved, and affectionately known as 'the galloper' in the navy. He was a good rider and as his name was originally Gilpin without the Brown he was dubbed a connection of the famous John Gilpin, which of course was quite untrue.[14] His wishes and ours did not coincide for he found London most unattractive, and it was a long time before he and my sister came to live there.

Vernon had now heard that he would be getting a job on the Imperial Defence Committee and this gave us a chance to look ahead and feel more secure. So we decided to furnish a house of our own and regretfully said goodbye to the house where we had enjoyed a really lovely garden. Our new home was a pure and simple villa residence, very suburban, but quite comfortable, adequate enough while Vernon was working in London. He would get back on Saturdays and get plenty of tennis and golf, which kept him fit. In summer he got several weeks' leave which we often spent in Ireland, sometimes it coincided with that of my brother-in-law Colonel Freeth, and he and his family would join up with ours making a real bear garden of our old home, but all the greatest fun. Fishing expeditions in the trout streams nearby generally ended with disappointed hopes of good fishing, but this did not damp the enthusiasm of any of the plans for better luck next time.

At home we had installed a German governess as we wanted our children to become proficient in foreign languages and thought it a good way to begin early with German. In August Vernon's favourite cousin married a German called Siebel though we were none of us very enamoured by the idea. We felt uneasy at the prospect, for there was continual sabre rattling at the Hohenzollern Court in Berlin, and Vernon thought things might be none too easy for his cousin if war were to break out. As a matter of fact during the First World War she was fairly safe with her large family of boys and girls, for the Germans had thoughtfully sent her husband to fight on the Russian border where he was away from any contact with the British. But things were very different in the Second World War when her four sons and sons-in-law were called up and had to fight against us. Eventually, when that war came to an end, our second son was with our army of occupation and was with the actual party near Dusseldorf which saw to it that this cousin's family were treated as people who could be trusted. A curious position for them, to have 'enemy' officers billeted on them. There were some very sore feelings, but on the whole things worked out well.

17

NEW PLANS

❖

But to go back to the year 1908, Vernon was asked to take the mailbag as King's Messenger to Berlin and St Petersburg and thought it would be amusing to go. So in September he started off for Berlin and after visiting the embassy left for St Petersburg. Here he met again General Mojack our old friend of Shan-Hai-Kuan days. The General knew everybody in the Tsar's entourage, he was exceedingly circumspect, but was most expert in gaining the knowledge he needed to keep him abreast of the intimate governmental intrigues in which he probably played quite an important part. One night there was a big dinner to which Vernon was invited and his commentary in his diary was 'no end of a dull time' – so evidently everyone was being very careful to divulge nothing of what was going on, and there was much to hide in those restless days. It was a pleasanter evening when he went off to the opera to hear some lovely music that he enjoyed immensely. After a couple of days of sightseeing and meeting old friends at lunch and dinner he returned home having been ten days away. Again a comment in Vernon's diary which said, 'Settle up accounts at the Foreign Office. Whole trip cost £41 and I am only 2/6 out of pocket.' To compare expenses with those of the present day when a trip of that sort would cost four of five times as much, makes one realise what an utterly different world we live in now.

During the course of his work Vernon saw a good deal of the Japanese military attaché. He felt sure that friendship with Japan was a big national asset and when, in later years, we gave up our alliance with her soon after the end of the First World War, Vernon felt it was a tragic mistake, for Japan had fought gallantly by our side with her navy and had loyally backed our war efforts in every way. He foresaw the consequences that followed, for it became only too evident that the Japanese understood very clearly the motive that lay behind the breaking up of that alliance in spite of our assurances that it would make no difference to our friendly relations. As time went on those in the Japanese government friendly to the West were pushed out by the more ambitious commercial- and military-minded politicians who meant to make Japan a great independent power, mistress of the Far East, and who could defy the West and America should they attempt to curb her thrust towards Eastern domination. But, in those early days we were still on excellent terms with Japan and those in the saddle were of the old honourable type, very different to those who rose to power later on.

One of the questions constantly coming under review at the meetings of the Imperial Defence Committee was the need to form a system of counter-espionage, for there was a growing menace to the security of the country in the work of enemy agents carrying out enquiries into the secrets of our defences at the behest of certain foreign powers. It was causing great concern to both our naval and military Directors of Intelligence and it was imperative these espionage activities should be watched and countered. Colonel James Edmonds, as he then was, suggested that somebody suitable should be entrusted with the task of originating an effective scheme to check this dangerous spying, and he very quietly turned to Vernon, who was amazed to hear him put his name forward. Vernon had to think quickly. He knew that, should he accept the job that was now seriously offered to him, he would be running a great risk. He would have to retire, on paper though not in fact, to enable him to remain at the War Office without being moved from one place to another, which in the ordinary course of a soldier's life was inevitable. He might be a failure, and what then? He would be left jobless and to what else could he turn? Jobs were not easy to find. It is wonderful how confident and optimistic one can be, for when Vernon came to consult with me before taking this big step, I had not the slightest doubt that he would make a success of it and enthusiastically supported his wish to accept. So he made his decision and the work entrusted to him began. Just one man, and after a while, a second, a clerk, the request for whom was greeted with surprise by the authorities when their consent to such extravagance had to be obtained!

Soon things began to take shape and the foundations of what was to become a great department were laid. By the autumn of the year 1909, Vernon had left his ordinary army career and had started to collect information vital to our great official departments. He gradually but surely gained the confidence and goodwill of those he worked for. At first it was very uphill work, for it took much time and patience to sift what came in, and everything had to be absolutely foolproof before he could ask the necessary authority to give warrants to enable the police to make arrests. Those in authority had to be fully convinced that it was essential in the interests of the country that these arrests should be made.

Amongst the first few cases to be brought to trial was that of Lieutenant Helm.[1] It was in 1910 that Vernon heard it said that a man, possibly a German, was sketching near Portsmouth. He carried his sketching materials about with him quite openly, but seemed particularly interested in making very detailed drawings of the defences in that area. He was questioned and as he could give no satisfactory explanations of what he was doing he was arrested and proved to be a spy, but so inefficient that he was considered of little importance and was released. But this was a beginning. Vernon moved cautiously; he was aiming at gradually building up the channels by which a network at the centre could be created. He was often told by his friends that he would find himself thrown over if he were to make the slightest slip, but he carried on confidently, and now the first suspect had fallen into the net. It was a big moment, he had to investigate entirely alone, and make sure that the incriminating evidence would be found on the suspect himself. Well it was a success, all went as he had planned and he could score one up, sufficient reward for his efforts. He was keeping a very watchful eye on such places as Plymouth and Portsmouth. He heard that a man speaking English with a very guttural accent was the owner of a small yacht, *The Egret*, on which he seemed to be enjoying sailing on the River Yalm and round the coast near Falmouth. He spent money freely and was very hospitable – nobody bothered about him until some of the people he was constantly entertaining began to wonder why he seemed to be so interested in local naval and military matters. Vernon came to hear about this man whose name was Schultz and questioned some of the people who had been entertained by him.[2] On investigation he discovered that Schultz was receiving large sums of money from an agent employed by the German secret service. So far Schultz had been unable to get much information and his efforts betrayed that he himself had not much technical knowledge – but it was evidently hoped that facts of value to his employers would be forthcoming as soon as he became more expert at obtaining them. Vernon was collecting sufficient evidence to have him arrested, but Schultz was now aware that he was under suspicion and was getting into touch with a solicitor. It was of the utmost importance to arrest him with the incriminating information on him or in the cabin of the yacht where he was living. Vernon knew that close to where the yacht was moored a certain field had to be crossed and fortunately for him a flock of sheep was grazing quite near. Just as the police and Vernon were approaching the boat they saw the solicitor making for a boat at the same spot. The sheep rushing away from them impeded the solicitor and he, waving them away, got thoroughly mixed up with them, for they were careering first one way then another, till Vernon's boat had got well away and Schultz was arrested in time. It had been most exciting at the last moment, poor Schultz looked very crestfallen and smiled sadly at the baffled solicitor. Later Schultz was tried and convicted.

From that time on things began to move, and it soon became necessary to have an assistant – Captain Frederick Stanley Clarke[3] was the first officer to come and help, and then later came Captain RJ Drake,[4] a most able man and most successful sleuth, small hope for anyone who fell into his net. Those were exciting days, for always it was a thrill watching and waiting to see if they were following up the right trails and would find their man. One false step would crash the whole delicate set-up, and leave the officers stranded. Vernon was now always alluded to as 'K', and his department was quickly increasing in importance.[5] The choice of suitable men who wished to join the staff of what was called the Security Service, and later MI5, was necessarily somewhat restricted. It was now evident that Vernon needed the services of an expert legal adviser to keep them all working strictly legally and, in fact, to create the fabric on which the whole legal side of the work would have to rest. Walter Moresby, son of Admiral John Moresby, was a very astute barrister and under his guidance the many legal pitfalls that might have trapped them were avoided.[6]

In 1911 Vernon was asked to go on the Prince Henry Tour. This was a car-testing tour in which Prince Henry of Prussia took a great interest.[7] He considered that the tour would increase their knowledge of our British methods of business and give them an idea of local colour. It was July and Vernon, who felt the tour would give him a short holiday and might be amusing, went off to Hamburg accompanied by another officer who spoke German fluently, and together they arrived at the dock where the cars were to be shipped for England. The German cars were magnificent specimens and they certainly made a great impression on their arrival at such places as Stratford-on-Avon, Welbeck Abbey, Chatsworth and many of our big midland towns. The Germans were everywhere, entertained with much hospitality at the best hotels.

Finally they came to London where the RAC gave them a banquet.[8] I was there with Vernon and heard a really delightful speech by Prince Henry in appreciation of all that had been done for them. The people at our table, rich German merchants with their wives, were not as complimentary as their prince. They expressed themselves heartily sick of the menus for lunches and dinners to which they had been invited; it did not seem to occur to them that their opposite English neighbours could talk German and might understand their grouses. 'Always salmon wherever we go,' they said, and perhaps it really was a bit lacking in imagination on our part that in trying to give them the best we had, most hotels had had the same bright ideas! Many wondered very much why the tour had been planned, and, as the war broke out so few years afterwards, people thought it might have been a case of spying out the land. However, as all the Germans we saw were dyed-in-the-wool business people, and completely unmilitary, it did not seem likely. Vernon enjoyed it all as a pleasant holiday, for it certainly was that, and went back to his work again, which was becoming more absorbingly interesting every day.

Vernon was finding it necessary to engage an increasing number of clerks and women to run a registry where there was a system of card indexing which gradually produced an enormous collection.[9] He had a firm feeling that there were only a few years in hand to enable them to be prepared for the war that he felt was surely and steadily approaching. And how right he was. He had a wonderful flair for organising, coupled with the gift of making people work together happily and smoothly. He was laughingly called 'the man with the golden tongue' for he certainly was diplomatic and tactful to an unusual degree. He always knew how to time his requests to the various heads of the great state departments he had to deal with, to ensure that his ideas of what could further the work should be treated with understanding and his requests granted. And he had much to ask, some of it a very new departure, but he was never refused, for he became completely trusted. It took, of course, years of successful work to bring this absolute confidence to fruition. In the meantime several suspicious foreigners had been discovered prying into matters of military concern, which could only be accounted for by their thirst for information of use to potential enemies. Most of them, or more truly all of them, seemed to be working as paid agents of Germany. Their methods were various, some clumsy and fairly harmless, others were very cleverly thought out and difficult to expose.

I have mentioned the Helm case: not very important, the man who had been making sketches of Portsmouth defences; also that of Schultz, caught near Plymouth and now brought to trial – nothing more was heard of him. Other cases soon followed.

There were rumours about a man convicted of fraud in the Far East – a German, said to be a marine captain, a likely person to undertake any unpleasant job after his long sentence of penal servitude, especially if a German agent should offer good money for the job.[10] He was carefully watched and found working under orders from people interested in serving German secret agents. He used a special code, which was sufficient evidence of his activities. He was arrested and given a further taste of penal servitude. Naturalised Englishmen, originally Germans, were especially under suspicion, and it was found that they were most active in discovering people who bore a grudge against society. These were of low morality, or drunkards of a bad type, down and outs generally, who might be clever enough to be trusted with jobs sufficiently well paid to keep them working, and who were unlikely to sell the pass while it was worth their while to continue in spite of the risks they ran. If they were successful the pay increased very considerably. Another method that enemy agents employed to gain their ends was to offer small weekly sums of money to men in our services to report quite harmless small talk in their barracks or on the lower deck of HM ships, just to provide friendly gossip in foreign newspapers interested in the British way of life. It was hoped that gradually innocent correspondents would write more confidential details and slide down the slippery slope of giving away items of news useful to the enemy secret agents. Naturally our Security Service took special care to prevent any success in this direction.

A name, Rodriguez, kept on cropping up while investigations were being made; nothing really incriminating could be discovered about him but it seemed strange that men answering to his description seemed to be active in various ports of particular interest.[11] Such names as Alberto Rossi, Garcia, Harry Ford, Robert Wilson, H Ellison and Harry Marbay were found to all be the same man. He changed his name with each change of address and was eventually arrested in Portsmouth and ordered to be deported.

As methods of counter-espionage improved some very tricky cases were exposed. One was of a man in our own navy.[12] He was an

Englishman highly trusted with very secret technical information which enemy agents would give very large sums of money to obtain, so far quite impossible in our Service. This was the only case Vernon ever had to deal with in the navy. This man, free and easy as are most naval men, seemed to be altering in character: no longer gay but reserved, uneasy, curiously unlike himself. It was noted that he was receiving letters from abroad, seemed rather flush with money and most certainly worth watching. He covered up his tracks most carefully, but those hoping to expose him were more skilful than he was at evading them. It was a most exciting chase, had it not been so tragic. It was found that he was receiving large sums of money and giving away very valuable information. It came as a horrible shock to those who knew, that an Englishman would be found selling his own country. He was arrested in London and given a heavy sentence of penal servitude. It was always a difficulty under our existing laws, so fair to the possible lawbreaker, to bring suspects before the courts, unless the case against them was so complete as to warrant an arrest. Later, an alteration of the law made it possible for the authorities to arrest on suspicion under certain safeguards and only with the approval of the Director of Public Prosecutions. This Security Service could, of course, make no arrests, but had to prepare each case with the utmost care so as to present it leaving no doubt as to the intentions of the person suspected, and these intentions had to be sufficiently serious to be considered dangerous to the security of the country. When the information had all been collected and sifted and the case ready to be sent up to the Director of Public Prosecutions, he would, if he thought sufficiently incriminated, issue a warrant for the arrest of the suspect. When Sir Basil Thomson was the head of Scotland Yard, Vernon and he had many plans to make together, for his men had to make the arrests and events were often very exciting.[13]

It was in 1912 that the awful *Titanic* disaster horrified the world. That ship, the very latest in design and with every comfort and luxury that could be thought out for a transatlantic liner, went down on her maiden voyage, for she had crashed into an iceberg, barely visible till it was too late. My father, who was the agent for the White Star Line to which the

Titanic belonged, had only a day or two before that shaken hands with the proud captain of this magnificent vessel, when she called at Queenstown on her voyage to New York. He was heartbroken, so many of his friends were on board and the ship carried a full complement of passengers. Some of them were saved, but oh so few; the horror of it still comes back as I write about it.

Vernon was in Glasgow when this news came through; he was investigating the Graves case, which entailed much preparation. Armgaard Karl Graves was arrested; another success to be scored.[14] He was just going to skip out of the country, the chase was a hot one. Would the code they were certain was concealed on him be found in time? They searched his belongings; it was exciting, it always was exciting, this end of the trail after ceaseless work had left no other conclusion than that he was a spy. They found the incriminating document very cleverly concealed on his person and the arrest followed. Had they been mistaken and the document not discovered it would have put the detectives in a very awkward position and their search made to look like unwarrantable interference in the affairs of an innocent man. But Vernon's information was as near foolproof as possible, he made no slips. Graves was sentenced to eighteen months' imprisonment. The authorities were beginning to realise that enemy agents were extremely active and that the department known as MI5 was getting to grips with them.

18

SOME FRUITION

❦

Looking through Vernon's diary of the following year, 1913, I read 'Saw Pegoud loop the loop.'[1] Brooklands, quite close to where we lived in Weybridge and constructed by the private enterprise of Mr HF Locke King at the cost of over a quarter of a million pounds, and enthusiastically and financially assisted by his wife, was becoming famous as a track for racing motorists and those very rare people, the flying pioneers.[2] Pegoud, the French airman, having looped the loop with his crazy-looking plane in France, came over to Brooklands to repeat this wonderful performance. Vernon and I were thrilled watching him, and it was only a short time previously that we had seen Bleriot fly over to Brooklands after he had made the first flight across the Channel.[3] Soon we had one of our own flyers showing us what an English plane could do, and Hamel, an enthusiastic young flyer, gave a demonstration which was a splendid effort.[4] When we look back now at what was achieved with those early planes, we wonder at the courage of the pilots taking such amazing risks in those rickety machines. Brooklands was fast becoming a great centre of attraction – for motor racing was very popular, and considering the speeds that cars could reach in those days Brooklands track, though small, was quite adequate. Vernon and I were watching the racing on one occasion when we suddenly saw one of the cars leap up the high banking of the track and crash straight into the woods outside. Something had gone wrong with the engine and the car literally flew into the trees. The driver was unconscious for many months but otherwise only slightly hurt; he recovered but his mind was a complete blank as to what had happened during the whole of that day.

Vernon's diary, which he wrote up carefully, kept track of every interesting event but was never in the least indicative of his work, for it was a point of honour with him that nothing should ever be recorded in it. Even when he had to make appointments to meet people of great importance connected with the investigations that he was constantly making, there was nothing to indicate the where, the why, or the wherefore in these diaries. Everything had to be done unobtrusively and when cases in which he was interested came up for trial there was never any mention of his department in the accounts given in the press; his requests that this should be so were always honoured. There were, however, a very few exceptions and it is from some of these accounts which had actually been reported that I can touch upon individual cases. Some of the most thrilling of them all were heard on camera. What tales must be locked away in the official archives.

Just now Vernon had heard of a man, a very military-looking figure, who was said to be travelling for an American firm of music publishers.[5] He was accompanied by a woman who approached certain people in London; they seemed to be regularly employed by German agents under cover of quite innocent small trading.[6] Their correspondence seemed not quite in keeping with their business contacts and they were worth watching. The lady, in a very ingratiating manner, was offering some rather catchy songs to one of these traders; he seemed interested though he did not sell music. Having left the songs in the shop she went off to a rendezvous with the man of very military bearing. It was discovered that he was an officer in the German Army and through the agency of the shopkeeper had delivered a message in code, discovered in the songs when a search was made. It was now pretty clear that one of the methods of obtaining and sending information used by the headquarters of the German secret service was to find Germans, or Germans who were now naturalised British subjects, who could be trusted to become distributing centres. Correspondence intended for their agents working in this country were sent to them and they acted, so to speak, as post boxes.[7] One such was a little hairdresser, Gustav Ernst by name.[8] He was in a small way of business and little known – but he was very useful to those who did not wish to appear to be sending letters too frequently to the same addresses. Ernst received packets of correspondence, which he had to stamp and repost in this country. Once this was discovered it became useful to know of these so-called post boxes to those hoping to frustrate the plans of enemy agents.

I remember that on one occasion a curious-looking man came to our house in Weybridge. I was at home getting ready to go out when there was a ring at the door. I had heard heavy footsteps coming up the gravel path and wondered whose tread that could be, when I listened to the maid being asked by someone with a very guttural foreign accent if Captain Kell was in. The answer was no, but that his wife could see him if he wished. I looked out and there stood a tall brusque figure, who had a most abrupt manner; he answered rudely that he would see no one but Captain Kell, and walked away with a tread so military that I seemed to see the goose step and hear the barking orders of a Prussian officer. I could never trace who he was or why he came; a German he must have been, and on some sort of spy errand. He had certainly not tried to be at all ingratiating, and if a spy, a very ham-handed one. But that was the only time that anyone of suspicious nature came as far as the actual house we lived in. I know of no one else.

In 1912 Vernon had to make enquiries about a case in Ireland and on going to Dublin met Neville Chamberlain and James Dougherty of the USA, lunching with them at the Kildare Hotel.[9] In the days before the Free State was created, and later the Republic, Dublin was a delightful place to stay in; some people will say that it is just as gay now as it was then, but I wonder if that can be true. There was such a sense of carefree enjoyment, especially at the Viceregal Court – the arts flourished in theatre and concert halls, there was always a welcome for sport at its best – the gaiety was infectious and hard to recapture now. Vernon enjoyed every moment of his visit and after his work was accomplished he left for the south where my sister, Ruth Freeth, with her family, and I, with mine, had descended upon my uncomplaining parents in our beloved home at Westlands, Queenstown. Vernon could only stay a few days and when he got back to London he was offered the job of Chief Constable of the Metropolitan Police, but his own work was much too enthralling to think of that. He was following up several tracks that might lead to important developments concerning people who, if not rendered harmless now, would give an immense amount of trouble later on.

One case was of a very charming woman – good-looking, intelligent, who was of foreign nationality. She attracted the attention of those trained to watch by the rather effortless way she moved her arm, which was encased in plaster and in a sling, very professionally tied up. She was followed as she walked towards the train, for she had just taken a ticket for a town in the Rhineland. A man stepped up to her and very courteously asked her to come with him to see someone who wanted to speak to her. Momentarily startled, she quickly regained her composure and gaily smiled at her very courteous companion and seemed quite reassured by his politeness. On being taken into a room and her arm examined, it was discovered after removing the plaster that the tight bandage underneath contained important information very useful to the German secret service. As for the so-called broken arm? Well, it proved to be perfectly sound! She took it quite calmly that her ruse had failed and also the arrest which followed.

On another occasion, a woman arrived at Dover wearing a very pretty bunch of artificial flowers. As it was the time of year when fresh flowers were in profusion one of our agents wondered why the bunch was artificial and asked her to step into a room nearby. Cunningly hidden inside the stems of the flowers was a message to be given to an enemy agent over here. It was impossible to keep up the pretence that she did not know that her flowers were anything other than a kindly gift from a friend – and she was given a sentence, when tried, which kept her under lock and key for a long time. Women were occasionally used by the Germans as agents if they were possessed of a ready wit and adept at using it when in a tight corner. But their usefulness was somewhat limited.

It was strenuous work, this planning and counter-planning for Vernon and his staff, and a short holiday was imperative especially in the autumn after months of exacting work. So he decided to go to Switzerland to Beatenberg on Lake Thun, and we were lucky in the weather for the first few days of our visit. The lake was unbelievably blue, with the autumn tints of the trees all along the shore mirrored in the water; tints of brilliant red and gold, very beautiful in the bright sunshine, enhanced by the azure blue of the lake. We gazed absolutely entranced – here was a world of beauty remote from the hustling, scheming of the world we had left behind. One forgot, for the moment, the sinister impressions left by the discovery of the cunning plots to help in planning aggressive wars and ruin the peace that each country tried to guard so preciously. For the moment, anyway, Vernon could relax and be refreshed by the beauty and peace around him. The weather changed after a couple of days and we were wrapped in a blanket of mist and fog, and after waiting impatiently for it to lift we decided to leave Beatenberg and go up the Rigi Mountain to the Kulm Hotel where, however, we found it just closing till the winter season should begin. So we decided to camp ourselves in a little hotel at Rigi Staffel which was rather primitive, but clean, and run by delightful people, very welcoming and ready to please. The food was quite adequate, and the beds comfortable, if you did not mind feather beds over you and under you; Vernon slept well in this feather bedding, but I couldn't.

We went out for rather limited walks. Though short, they were lovely, for we were well above the cloud that was stretched out below us like an enormous billowing blanket reaching halfway up the mountains, and at sunset the effect of these clouds, rosy tipped and golden, was wonderful to see. For nearly a week it remained like this and then, one afternoon as we sat on a seat provided for those climbers who came up to see the view from a spur of the mountain, we suddenly saw a tiny speck push through the cloud, then another one, and we realised that we were looking at the twin towers of the Lucerne Cathedral. Very slowly the blanket of cloud drifted away and then, in the dazzling sunshine of that afternoon, the panorama of the lake and surrounding countryside unfolded before us, shimmering in the light and indescribably beautiful. Gradually the light faded, the sun was setting and we hurried back to our hotel. The next day there was a very cold wind with snow and rain, so we decided to go to Berne, and after a day or two of sightseeing in that lovely town we returned to London where Vernon found plenty of work awaiting him and I went back to our house in Weybridge.

It was towards the end of that year 1912 that Captain Eric Holt-Wilson came to reinforce the staff of officers that was gradually being enlarged to deal with the expansion that was taking place in the work.[10] He was a man of almost genius for intricate organisation; his work of planning every detail with infinite foresight of what would be needed to meet the constant increase in size and importance of a department like MI5 contributed in large measure to its smooth running. Not only was he a most valuable officer but he was an intensely loyal and devoted friend, and Vernon found in him the support that is so important when work such as his caused him anxiety and strain. He could always rely on his ready cooperation. Captain Holt-Wilson did not actually start work till January of the following year, 1913.

It was in February that we heard of the terrible disaster to the Scott expedition to the South Pole. Scott and his companions gave us an example of endurance, heroism and courage of such high order that it drew the admiration of the whole world. There had been such high hopes of that expedition and now here was failure, but failure that had such greatness to redeem it. In that year there was a feeling of uneasiness all over Europe, for the sabre rattling in Germany was becoming more and more aggressive. We were at last looking to our defences, even in our small village of Oatlands, as in villages all over England they were getting together on the subject of home defence. People realised that war seemed inevitable, and that if it came, we were in no way prepared for it. The idea of an invasion had seemed as remote as if we lived on another planet, but now we asked ourselves if it was wise to carry on as if we were in the peaceful atmosphere of the Victorian age. Our village did some training in rifle firing, but little more than that – we were certainly due for the rude awakening, which came later on. We had a big parade of National Reservists, also a prize-giving day at the rifle range, the prizes being distributed by General Sir Lyttelton-Annesley who lived near Weybridge and took what interest he could in the local activities.[11]

Towards the end of 1913 Vernon was promoted to Major; his work was meeting with success and more and more officers and staff were required. The Security Service MI5 was thoroughly established, and the other government departments: Naval, Military, Home Office and Foreign Office, gave their ready cooperation with whatever was required to further its effective planning. There was no doubt that Vernon had gained the goodwill of all concerned in his work, and this was greatly contributing to its success.

His diary in early 1914 just touches on the efforts being made to locate every individual who might be a danger to the security of the country. In some port towns, such as Folkestone, the hotels would be filled with guests of many nationalities and some of them interested MI5. One such seemed evasive in his replies to questions. He was in the habit of frequenting small shops in back streets – sweet shops where he bought chocolates attracted him. He was a gruff, burly foreigner, strange that he should like to eat chocolates as he sat on a seat tucked away in a quiet corner of the seashore. Why should he want to go so far from town to enjoy the chocolates? There was nothing else in his behaviour that attracted the attention of those who were quick to detect anything unusual about him yet they were persuaded that sooner or later the man would give himself away. They noticed that he received parcels from abroad, and they wondered if he sent any from the small post offices he used to post his letters. One day he actually did post a small parcel and some of our agents abroad were asked to look into that fact, for it certainly seemed that it was chocolates that were being sent. The chocolates were carefully scrutinised and there, tucked away among them, was one which seemed to be filled with cream, but concealed in the cream was a neatly folded tiny message. It gave important information! So the long-expected giveaway had come at last. On being confronted with the message the German agent tried to bluff his way out of his dilemma but of course it was no good, and one more spy was put under lock and key. It was discovered that such messages were sometimes concealed under postage stamps and some were written in invisible inks and spread through shorthand letters, in code requiring great ingenuity to discover – but MI5 were getting wise to all the tricks and were generally one jump ahead. One rather curious one was a telegram which read: 'Father dead, await instructions,' which was turned into: 'Father deceased, what action?' Back came a wire: 'Father dead or deceased, please explain?'[12] Evidently some of these messages were puzzling even to their intended recipients. Another one was a map of a well-known town, and along the tram routes was a message in Morse code which was further complicated by the alphabet being used in shifting positions, such as the first letter being altered to the fifth or sixth position and so on. The methods of these agents grew more ingenious as time went on and they were carefully watched. On the outbreak of war many of them who had purposefully not been arrested, being useful in uncovering further contacts, were immediately dealt with and put into safe custody.

19

WAR

✤

I t seems strange to think how carefree a life most of us were living as summer came in 1914; we were so unprepared and optimistic, a national characteristic which seems frequently to bring us to such a fantastic danger point.

Vernon, feeling as he had done ever since 1909 that war was inevitable, geared up his organisation to be fully prepared for whatever emergency might arise. When the famous Sarajevo incident took place and the murder of Archduke Franz Ferdinand led to war being declared between Austria and Serbia, he knew the fuse had been lit, and awaited the explosion that followed so shortly after that horrible assassination.[1]

Vernon left Weybridge and came to live permanently in London. Captain Haldane, cousin of Lord Haldane, joined his staff which needed men of exceptional ability, for their work, if successful, would be of major importance when war actually broke out.[2] At first Vernon slept in his office with many telephones around his bed, but that was only prior to the whole scheme coming into action which had all been so carefully planned to meet the outbreak of the war.

On August 4th, when war was declared, every suspect was put into safe custody with one exception.[3] He got away, but his information was evidently so slender that the Germans did not know for a whole fortnight that any British troops had landed in France, and a fortnight's ignorance of such vital information at the commencement of a campaign such as the Germans had planned made an enormous difference to their calculations. It was therefore quite a considerable victory for us that they knew nothing of our troop movements for all that time. The precautions that it was necessary to take to prevent spies entering our country or from leaving it with dangerous information were at once put into operation, entailing constant supervision at the ports and watching along the coasts. Some spies actually did get in, but the organisation to deal with them worked well and rather rueful admiration that was expressed by the head of the secret service in Germany itself bore eloquent testimony to its efficacy. The war went forward with many bitter disappointments for us, especially when we heard of the loss of three of our cruisers hit by German submarines. We had always thought of our navy as quite invincible, an opinion shared by most of the general public, and we now realised that the submarine menace was going to require almost superhuman efforts to defeat. These efforts were made and with the splendid assistance of the merchant navy, the dangers and trials that might so easily have defeated the best-laid plans of our three services were overcome by the gallantry of the sailors and their skill in manoeuvring the diminishing fleets of ships at their command.

Our 'contemptible little army' so looked down upon by Kaiser Bill was doing heroic deeds but required men and ever more men. Without conscription we could never get enough of them. The posters displayed on all the hoardings with Lord Kitchener's face looking forcefully at us and calling for recruits had brought in a great voluntary army, but all these efforts would have been infinitely more effective had they been planned, years before, to meet an emergency.[4]

In October came the tragic news of the death of the only son of the chief of one of our intelligence departments.[5] Father and son were in France, travelling in a speeding car which skidded into a tree, overturned and pinned down the father by the leg. He could see his son lying mortally injured but could not get near him. Frantically he took out his penknife and tried to saw away his ankle to get free, but to no avail. He was found later badly hurt, a gallant naval man of great courage.[6]

The war dragged on wearily enough for us while our new armies were in the making. The French were taking terrible blows, losing the very flower of their manhood in battles causing enormous casualties.

The work of the MI5 was bearing fruit and the net was spreading. It caught up one very smiling young man who arrived at one of our ports. When his turn came to have his luggage opened it was noticed that a shaving set he had with him was rather remarkable for with it was a bottle of lemon juice known by his interrogators as useful to bring out invisible inks. The young man seeing a look of suspicion cross their faces said brightly, 'I like using lemon juice after shaving.'[7] But they were not satisfied and searched further. The handle of the shaving brush proved to be hollow and inside, rolled up very neatly, was a blank piece of tissue paper and a small pen. On applying the lemon juice a message from the German secret service was deciphered, one of great importance. The smiling young man turned pale when asked why a pen was concealed with the paper, and could think of no reply. He paid dearly for his failure; one more of Steinhauer's agents was accounted for.

Steinhauer, himself the Chief of the German secret service, often visited this country.[8] His real name was Reimer, and he was clever and resourceful.[9] He tried to outwit Vernon's counter measures by every manoeuvre he could think of, but always the battle of wits went against him. Vernon had felt certain that Steinhauer had planted a sufficient number of agents here to be ready to give the vital information needed by the German general staff when the war broke out and was well prepared to counter it.

One of Steinhauer's agents, the man I previously mentioned, Karl Ernst, who ran a barber's shop in the Caledonian Road, London and acted as a 'post box' for receiving letters, was very successfully delivering letters in batches to enemy recipients. These had been sending them out of the country for use by the German secret service. Little did Steinhauer guess that the contents of the letters were known by those whose job it was to render the information that they contained harmless. Vernon managed to be always a move ahead of whatever was planned by Steinhauer and his staff of really able men. Most of the agents employed by the Germans worked only for the money they gained and were regarded with utter contempt, but the fine patriotism which prompted some of the men sent from Germany itself to endeavour to extract information vital to the success of their plans were of a totally different stamp. One such really fine man was Carl Lody, Senior Lieutenant of the German Naval Reserve.[10] He was caught, brought to trial and found guilty. He wrote a letter to the Commanding Officer in Wellington Barracks where he was confined, to thank him for the courtesy and consideration with which he had been treated by those in charge of him before he was shot. Here indeed was a man who had undertaken a job which must have been very foreign to his nature, from purely patriotic motives. Vernon felt it deeply that so brave a man should have to pay the death penalty for carrying out what he considered to he his duty to his country.

Many years later a tribute to Carl Lody appeared in a German newspaper in which it was stated that he had offered his services to the Admiralty staff on hearing that it was clear 'that the German Supreme Command had no knowledge whatever of the despatch or the movements of the British Expeditionary Force.' Since Lody, owing to a severe operation, could not offer his services as a fighting man at the front, he asked to be employed by the Admiralty intelligence staff. Then followed a long account of what he had done in espionage work and his eventual arrest. The legal proceedings, when he was brought before a court martial, were described as worthy of British justice, and a pattern of impartiality. In his farewell letter to his family he ended with these words: 'It is a great consolation to me that I am not being treated as a spy. I have had upright judges and will die as an officer and not as a spy. Farewell – God bless you.'

During 1914 and 1915 we were passing through some very bitter days, waiting anxiously for a turn of the tide, which was long in coming. It was in May 1915 that the Germans torpedoed and sank the *Lusitania*.[11] It came as a great shock, for we had felt sure that the Germans would never wish to antagonise the Americans by endangering the lives of their passengers travelling in British ships to and from America.

The Germans had repeatedly warned New York that the crack ship *Lusitania* would be torpedoed if she came across on the advertised date, but nobody took it too seriously. It was felt that this ship would be so carefully guarded that she would be the safest ship to travel in. It was therefore a stunning blow both to the Americans and ourselves when we heard that the *Lusitania* had been torpedoed off the Old Head of Kinsale on the south coast of Ireland. My sister, wife of Colonel George Freeth, was a VAD in a branch at Queenstown, Cork Harbour. She was living with her family in my parents' house, while her husband was serving in France.[12] Admiralty House was the centre of activity, for neither the Free State, nor the Republic of Eire were yet in being. My sister and all those who were trained in Red Cross work were at once asked to help, and she described the events of that fateful day as follows:

As soon as the news of the sinking flashed along the coast, all was got ready to receive the survivors as the rescuing craft brought them into Queenstown. Everyone wished to give all assistance they could. I myself had just previously been attending a meeting of the Soldiers and Sailors Families Association which deals with applications for help from those whose men were serving in the forces. We discussed a rumour that a German submarine was hiding in a cove not far from Kinsale, and had advertised her presence by sinking a small ship laden with bricks. We argued that the Admiralty knew of the danger and had advised the great liner to take a zigzag course. Just then we received the message, 'All VADs wanted at once,' and knew Lusitania must have been hit. I got into my uniform and was soon joining those watching tensely for the first survivors to be brought in. Destroyers and other boats had been sent to look for them, and the rescuers as they approached the scene of the disaster were amazed to see what they thought were bobbing heads floating in the water; hundreds of them, but alas, they were dead bodies, legs uppermost! The lifesaving jackets that all these people were wearing were of a new pattern and fatal to any wearer jumping into the water from a height. They had kapok cushions back and front and these were forced up breaking the necks of the hapless wearers.

As the vessels picked up the dead and the living they found the latter were those who had slipped off the decks as the ship sank and they were level with the water. The crews in the destroyers gave very literal first aid, for they placed many apparently dead people on their sides, propping their mouths open with matches and indeed many were found to be still breathing and artificial respiration brought them back to life.

We, who were waiting in the little town to help those who were being brought in, were horrified at their pitiable condition. One of them, a young pregnant woman who eventually came back with me to our house, said she had not tried to get into the boats but had managed to hold on to some floating object to which others were also clinging. She was rescued after two hours and it was wonderful to hear later on that her baby had arrived safely and that she too was quite alright.

There was another woman well known in America and in London who, with her husband, was bringing her whole family to England. She had two older daughters, twin younger daughters, a boy of eight and a baby of six months, accompanied by a nanny and governess. The twin girls and governess who had been put into one of the boats by the husband were lost, but the others were gradually found in various parts of the town. The mother was most grateful for everything that had been done for her and felt that it was indeed wonderful that so many of her family had been rescued. One pathetic little figure standing bewildered amongst all the wet and miserable people awaiting accommodation was asked his name. John, was the reply – but John what? He did not know, but asked piteously for his mother who could not be found. He was only one of many sad cases – distracted parents looking for their children, searching every corner of the town. The little cemetery down in the valley behind the hilly town was now to have two enormous graves where hundreds of the dead were reverently laid and where relatives could come and find the last resting place of their loved ones, looked after with loving care.

There were many more instances of tragedy and great bravery in my sister's account but it has had to be curtailed.

Vernon wondered how this disaster would react on the American people. Would they accept it calmly or could it, at last, light the flame of anger that would change their neutral attitude into one of active participation in a war that was being fought in the cause of justice and freedom?

Everyone would work harder, even more willingly, over here to contribute towards the eventual victory, and in Vernon's office the enthusiasm increased. He had now been obliged to move his office to much larger premises to accommodate a very large staff. There were many women running the ever-expanding Registry. They were carrying our their duties most efficiently and the system on which they worked was most reliable. Miss Lomax was for many years the head of this section and her work was so excellent that Vernon could rest assured that whatever she, and those who worked with her and under her, were asked to do would be quickly and eagerly carried out.[13] If there was a rush they would gladly work all night if that would help towards the success of whatever job they had in hand. There was something personal in the ready response to what was asked of them, for Vernon had indeed the gift of inspiring those who worked for him, to give their best.

20

AIR RAIDS

❖

In November 1915 Vernon's father died very suddenly. It came as a great shock, for he had always seemed so cheery and gay. We did not know that, some little time before, he had had a heart attack and the doctor diagnosed angina pectoris. It seemed not to depress him at all and he carried on just as cheerfully as ever. Vernon had, of course, to see to everything for his stepmother, and to attend to the business side, which entailed much work. This, on top of his office work, which kept him at full stretch, was more than he could stand without a break, so he took a short holiday.

My youngest sister and her husband, Admiral Gilpin-Brown, who were at Admiralty House, Pembroke Docks, asked him and me to stay with them. Just before leaving London he and I went to His Majesty's Theatre to hear Ben Tillett speak,[1] the chair being taken at this meeting by the Duke of Rutland.[2] Ben Tillett was well known for his thumping oratory in the political cause of Labour, and was most eloquent but, on this occasion, he was bringing before his large audience the fact that we needed equipment for our troops at the front, for they had been rushed out with such haste that they had neither any suitable clothes to keep them warm in the trenches nor had they a sufficient supply of rifles and ammunition. A telling phrase was: 'Can you picture those men with nothing but their bare bodies to oppose to the guns of the enemy?' He spoke so well that the money for comforts for them poured out of the pockets of those tensely listening to him. Even jewellery was put into the collection, and the result was that work parties were started throughout the country to make shirts, knit socks, scarves and helmets: everything that could help the men suffering such hardships in the trenches. Never shall I forget the picture of Ben Tillett, very short of stature, and the Duke very long indeed, standing together side by side; one with an amused expression, the other looking down benevolently, and Ben Tillett saying that it was strange to find himself on the same platform as the Duke, who was poles asunder from him in his political views and yet completely at one with him at this time of dire need. Before very long in the following year, the supply of woolly things became too heavy to deal with. We heard that the troops were lining their trenches with scarves and cummerbunds, and the insects that they harboured were impossible to cope with. This may have been an exaggeration, but certainly 'the Sister Susies Sewing Shirts for Soldiers' worked with a will and later their energies were turned to equipping the Red Cross with much-needed hospital garments.

At Admiralty House, Vernon and I spent a very pleasant fortnight, and were there for the launching by my sister of submarine *J3*. It was an interesting ceremony, which went off without a hitch; the bottle hit the spot and broke in pieces and the ship slid down the ways with ease. We wished her much luck in the coming days when we knew she would have some desperate encounters.

In February of the following year, 1916, the Admiralty were very concerned over the question of the Zeppelin raids though, so far, they had not done much damage. But should they come near London and drop bombs there it would be most difficult to deal with. My cousin, Neville Usborne, of the Naval Air Service, was an inventor and sought some means of defeating the Zeppelin attacks.[3] He did, as he thought, perfect a method of firing into a Zeppelin from the air and tried it out with a naval friend as companion. The mechanism which had been made to use it failed through some mischance, on this occasion, and he and his friend crashed in their plane which fell like a stone to the ground, killing both men instantly. Admiral 'Jackie' Fisher, telegraphing to Neville's Osborne's parents, called it a major disaster.[4] He said the service had lost a fine officer whose inventions were of the greatest value to the navy. His brother, Cecil Vivian Usborne, also in the navy, was working on an invention intended to act as a protection to ships when in danger from mines.[5] He had, however, to leave his plans unfinished, having been ordered to take up another post where there were no facilities to help with his researches. Later they were to prove most useful in the working out of a really splendid method of submarine and mine detection invented by the then Commander Burney.[6] Cecil Vivien had previously invented a firing device known as 'the Usborne fall of shot' used throughout the navy, which greatly improved the accuracy of firing. He became a very well known personality in the service and reached the rank of Vice Admiral.

In the summer of 1916 Lord Kitchener and his staff set off in the cruiser HMS *Hampshire* to a secret destination. She never reached it, for she sank with all hands somewhere in the North Sea. Had a mine struck her or did a submarine get her? It was indeed a terrible disaster, and a triumph for the enemy. We regarded Lord Kitchener as one of the chief organisers of the plans for the eventual success of our arms. It was said that he and his staff had some very secret mission to perform, and if this was so those plans were now completely ruined. We faced the future with even grimmer determination and knew that those dread battles of 1916, with their fearful loss of life, could not be avoided. They were draining away the very lifeblood of the French and ourselves.

In June my brother-in-law, Colonel George Freeth, came over from France to an investiture where he was to receive a CMG. His family, who were living in my old home in Ireland, hurried over to greet him. A very happy photograph was taken of them at the gates of Buckingham Palace, his two little girls' eager faces as they looked at the decoration made such a pretty picture that it came out in the French newspapers with a caption describing the excitement of the children. They all came down to us at Weybridge, for I was holding the fort there and often coming up to London where Vernon was living at the Rubens Hotel. The Zeppelin raids were on and as yet we had not dealt with them sufficiently drastically to discourage them, but when we eventually brought down one after the other we hoped the danger was over, and Vernon decided to take a house in London where we could have the family with us.

The news of the death of one of his young cousins saddened us greatly – he had very reluctantly become a soldier for he was a very genuine pacifist. He had felt it his duty to join up, and trained sufficiently to be a really capable officer. He fell, leading his men over 'the top', shortly after his arrival in France. He had a premonition that he would not return, and told his father so. He was a fine man much misunderstood by those who had no patience with his outlook of genuine pacifism. The casualties at this time were indeed frightful and there was no break in the grim outlook.

In Vernon's office the strain of the work was beginning to tell on those who had been longest in the office and had very responsible jobs. Colonel Drake, the quickest witted and most successful frustrator of spies, had to take a short spell of sick leave, and many more were in need of a rest. Had there been greater success for our forces at the front it would have been much easier to bear the long strain, and though no one had the slightest doubt of the eventual outcome of the war, victory seemed long in coming. But success in the work of MI5 was very encouraging. Vernon was on the track of two Dutchmen. One had been a mate in a merchant ship, the other was an ex-AB in the Dutch Navy; they now called themselves commercial travellers and were selling cigars, quite successfully too, and seemed very keen businessmen. They had an elaborate price list giving many brands of excellent cigars. But somehow that price list caught the eye of those on the lookout for possible codes so frequently found hidden in the most unlikely places. Experts hunted through that price list for invisible ink disclosures and for various methods of conveying messages – there were so many new and ingenious devices being discovered every day. Cable censorship worked hard at it but no, all seemed perfectly above board. Vernon thought it was worth continuing a search for clues, and much time was expended on it. At last the secret of a most ingenious code was unearthed and it was found that these Dutchmen were collecting information on the number and disposition of certain ships in the navy. They had received very secret instructions from their employers, Steinhauer and his staff. They paid the penalty of their spying activities with their lives. Brave men certainly, but there was no patriotism in it nor even the love of adventure, however risky – it was all done for money and therefore Janssen and Roos were despicable men ready to do any dirty work merely for gain.[7]

Another so-called commercial traveller sold gas mantles.[8] He travelled about with a book called *Jane's Fighting Ships*. It gave a very comprehensive list of most of the ships in our navy, with a good many details concerning each one. Why this interest? This commercial traveller needed no information on our defensive forces in his way of business. So he was watched, and at first nothing suspicious could be detected. However, it was hoped that something would give him away eventually unless he really was just an interested inquirer admiring the number and quality of our ships. Then it was found that his passport was forged – it was an American passport – and this led those on the lookout to the discovery that Germans were using these forged American passports wholesale. The US government was accordingly notified and special precautions were taken to prevent this happening in future. The innocent commercial traveller was now trying to explain away a very incriminating fact that he carried a well-hidden code on his person. This proved to be most intricate and clever, and now his spying activities stood revealed. As it was wartime no prison sentence was given; spies knew that if caught they would have to pay the death penalty – and this man was tried, found guilty and executed.

With our armies growing ever larger all sorts of new training centres had to be provided, one of them being at Clare College, Cambridge. It was a strange picture entering the college and seeing men in khaki lying about on the lawns, never desecrated in such a manner when the undergraduates were up at Cambridge. There were army cooks installed in the great kitchen, in fact the whole place was now taken over by the army; the wonderful old dining hall was the officers' mess – what a change to see no caps and gowns, and khaki everywhere! In charge of this staff school was General Robert Hare: a most efficient officer, delightful to work for, an Irishman, and one of the most courteous of men. Vernon had to come up on duty and the Master of Caius invited him to stay when he was due to give a lecture to the officers. He asked me to come up with him and how greatly we enjoyed that visit. The Master of Caius lived in one of the oldest buildings in Cambridge, with a very special charm of its own. We forgot all the ugliness of war in those peaceful surroundings and I was very sad to leave it all behind when we returned to London.

21

RETURN TO LONDON

❧

Early in 1917 the family came up with me to live in London. I had at last found a house, after much searching, on Campden Hill. It was near some good day schools, which I needed for the two younger children. We came up from Weybridge on a cold snowy day, the furniture van sinking deep into the drive in front of our house. The maids got into the last van and thought it a huge joke; they brought our livestock with them – our beloved Scottie dog, the cat, and the parrot. A skid in the snowy road landed the van into a shop window on the way up, and slung the parrot cage through it, the screeching bird adding to the confusion. There was little harm done and the vans reached their destination without further mishap. On arriving at the house the wet snow and slush was brought inches deep into the newly cleaned house, and the kitchen had to be seen to be believed. My dauntless cook lit the kitchen fire and came to me in dismay to ask me to come and look at the flood. The boiler had burst and what was she to do next? There were the children to feed, and no means of cooking or of heating the water. Well somehow we all calmed down and things righted themselves sufficiently for us to do without the stove till workmen came the next day. We liked the house, and it was such a boon to have no more journeys to London and back to Weybridge. Vernon had got very tired of the Rubens Hotel with its very centrally heated atmosphere, though the manager and staff had spared no pains to make his long visit there as comfortable as possible.

Earlier that year Vernon heard he was to get the CB and in February he went to an investiture with his friend General Macdonogh, who was to receive his knighthood. We celebrated that event in very modest fashion, for the food situation was pretty difficult and no social occasions were easy to negotiate. We were all settling down nicely in our new house when air raids started up, with planes instead of Zeppelins. Frequently at night and punctually at dinnertime the maroons would go off, warning us of the approaching raid. I took the children downstairs to the basement till I found it more bother than it was worth, for the children were not the least alarmed and they were much better in bed. But our maids were really scared and would serve dinner with blanched faces, looking as if they longed to run away from it all. But they stuck to us and after time they too took but little notice of the raids.

In the summer when the holidays came and our elder son Jim was back from Oundle, his most excellent public school, we all went off to Whitby where we could get sailing and good bathing. As we were to stay in a house on the moors not too far away we got the benefit of both moor and sea air. Vernon joined us for a short time and friends of ours gave him some good salmon fishing which he greatly enjoyed, for he was most successful and landed some lovely fish. Just after he had gone back to London there was great excitement in Whitby, for a German submarine had come close in shore and shelled the ruins of Whitby Abbey – doing no further damage. We wondered if we were to expect a repetition of this sort of thing. Some of our small dirigibles called Silver Kings were sent up to keep a look out for enemy submarines but, as far as I know, there were no further raids on that part of the coast. There was great indignation at such useless destruction, for Whitby Abbey was a lovely ruin.

After the holidays our elder son went back to Oundle in School House where he was directly under that most remarkable headmaster, FW Sanderson.[1] Some have spoken of him as being the greatest headmaster since Dr Arnold.[2] He ran the school on very original lines. He had engineering workshops where the work executed by the boys was so accurate that some of it could be made use of, without question, to help the war effort. Sanderson was a man of rare ability and had a wonderful influence over boys. The classical side of the school was his special care and he was proud of the boys' records when they went up to the universities. He ran an excellent farming side, and a well-equipped scientific side. Opportunities to develop the artistic aspirations of boys who had a taste for music and painting were many – the concerts given at Oundle were quite outstanding – in fact this school was out to seek and develop whatever the boys were best fitted for. Vernon, who came with me to see the school on one occasion, went through the laboratories, the machine shops, the art rooms, and greatly admired the opportunities that these methods of such varied education gave to the boys but wondered how the cost of it was met. He was told that the money to set up the machinery for this very practical method of teaching was provided by the Grocers' Company in London, who generously supported the enthusiastic schemes of Mr Sanderson. His enthusiasm was certainly infectious, for parents as well as boys eagerly supported his ideals.

In London the air raids were becoming much more frequent, and on bright moonlit nights we feared the worst, for then the planes would come over in quite considerable numbers, and our reply to them was almost negligible. Our planes were not as swift as the Germans' and 'the Richthofen Circus', as it was called, could make short work of our very slow planes in the battle area.[3] In those days our young airmen's lives were of very short duration; they seldom lasted more than a fortnight, often much less. In spite of which there was never any lack of eager young men ready to try to be the lucky ones to gain an ascendency over the much more manoeuvrable German planes.

The war went dragging on – Vernon often wondered how much longer it would be before the end was in sight. We were steadily losing the very flower of our manhood, as were the French, and yet there was no sign that we were wearing down the enemy. On April 6th we seemed to reach the turning point, for it was then that the Americans came into the war. We knew now that we must win, for America could supply us with much that we were short of for munitions and her troops, fresh and eager, were there to reinforce our much-tried forces. Our food supplies were decreasing, and rationing had not yet been thought of. At last, when ships were being torpedoed in great numbers and out merchant fleet depleted, the authorities realised something must be done, and rationing began. We in London had no potatoes for many months, but we did have rice, and used that instead. Sugar also became very short, and we had a sort of substitute that cannot have been very healthy for it was all called in the very moment the war ceased. We ourselves got meat sent over to us from my people in Ireland, and what was most astonishing was that it would arrive alright; the postman would deliver a large joint at our door and say he hoped we'd have a good dinner! Seldom did we come up against any ill feeling amongst the shopping crowds. But once, when I was standing in a queue waiting for the family sugar ration, or so-called sugar, a woman in front of me pointed her finger over her shoulder at me and said to her friend, 'We's goin up, they's goin down.' Rather a curious way of describing the effort to give fair shares to everyone of what food was available.

That summer Vernon and I went off for his few days' leave to Dulverton in Somerset, and found that German prisoners of war were working in the garden of our hotel and in the fields helping the farmers. Vernon was much amused to see how perfectly happy they seemed, and that often the Germans would ride back on the farm horses while their masters walked beside them, chatting gaily. He asked about these men and was told that the farmers liked employing them, they were good workers: 'Never a straight back all day in the fields,' they said. They were decent lads, very different from some others who were truculent and difficult, the latter chiefly among those prisoners of war who were in camps where there was little or nothing for them to do.

When Vernon got back to London he was just in time to see the first big daylight raid. He was in his office but I, suddenly hearing the warning sounded, looked up to see the sky filled with droning planes, and heard explosions in quick succession. I was in a bus with my daughter and her cousin. We were on our way to the Prince's Theatre to a big demonstration organised by many schools, to give an exhibition of the Jaques-Dalcroze method of teaching concentration through rhythmic movements to music.[4] Some of these movements were on very lovely classical lines, some largely mathematical and were designed to promote the close attention of the children. When the bus driver realised what was happening, he pulled up his bus to the curb by Knightsbridge Barracks and everyone ran helter-skelter into the shops for shelter. After about half an hour we heard the maroons give the all-clear and we continued our journey through the streets where smoke was still rising from buildings hit by bombs in the Shaftesbury Avenue direction. We arrived safely at the Prince's Theatre and in fairly good time.

When Professor Jaques-Dalcroze stepped onto the platform and saw the whole theatre filled with schoolchildren he looked amazed, for all the schools expected had arrived with the exception of one: a well-placed bomb had blocked the railway station the children should have used to come up to London. Monsieur Jaques smiled, congratulated them all, and exclaimed, 'Ah, you have seen the Germans and have said, here they are, we will ask them to tea.' He did not think the English children as artistic as some of the children he had to deal with in Switzerland and in other parts of Europe, but he was immensely impressed by their calmness and cheerfulness and gave them every encouragement during their demonstrations of his rhythmic exercises.

We had plenty more raids after this one. They did not do much damage though there were some horrible incidents such as the complete destruction of the lovely Charles II house in the grounds of the Royal Hospital Chelsea, when an entire family was wiped out, with the exception of one child at school in the country. These raids took place mostly at night by moonlight and consequently when there was no moon we thought we were safe from attack. But on one particular night a most wonderful aurora borealis lit up the sky which was almost as bright as day and the Germans took advantage of this and came over, doing much more damage than usual.

In the summer of 1917 Vernon received the KBE and later was given the Belgian Order of Leopold, the Order of St Olaf from Norway, the Order of St Lazarus from Italy and was made officer of the Legion of Honour, all in recognition of his work. It was bringing rewards, but Vernon regarded these as a thank you to his staff and to all who worked with him. He was most conscious and very proud of their untiring efforts to make a success of whatever work they set out to do. All those at the War Office who were dealing with military intelligence, such men at the head as General Sir George Macdonogh and Brigadier-General Sir George Cockerill,[5] gave him their unstinted support and he could always reckon on the willing cooperation of the Director of Naval Intelligence.[6]

In November of that year there was the following entry in Vernon's diary, just a few words: 'Break through Hindenburgh line.' At last the news was better, but there were to be many more months of severe fighting before the longed-for armistice could be signed. In December came the news of the death of a cousin, Fairfax Mackeson, a lieutenant in a destroyer. There was naval tradition in his blood, for he was the great grandson of Admiral of the Fleet Sir Fairfax Moresby and grandson of Admiral John Moresby.[7] He was a keen and most efficient officer, and one night his ship had to pick up her mooring in harbour – no lights allowed of any sort and the night was pitch black. There was a heavy sea running and the ship's cable had to be secured to the ring of the buoy. Fairfax Mackeson was lowered onto the buoy wearing a lifebelt and secured by a rope. He succeeded in fastening the ship's cable, but when the rope was pulled up the lifebelt was empty. It was presumed that he had been crushed between the ship and the buoy in that heavy sea. We were very proud of him. How many such gallant acts could be recorded, which no one will ever hear of, for they are all carried out in the ordinary course of duty.

MI5 were now investigating a very interesting case, for a different method of spying was being tried by the Germans. They were utilising naturalised British citizens to forward certain information if their plans were to prove fruitful. They obtained the services of a woman married to a German who was naturalised and by virtue of her marriage with this British subject she could live here under the cloak of his nationality. She was, however, separated from her husband. An ex-German officer living in the USA came over to work with this woman, and posed as representing a firm of music publishers and dealers in the USA. He was, as it happened, a really gifted musician. He arranged for the woman to do the travelling and in the meanwhile, though ostensibly offering music for sale, was to collect all the information that her instructors had asked her for. The ex-German officer was to send on any information in secret invisible ink messages. But they did not get far with their plans; they were allowed enough rope to establish their guilt unanswerably and then arrested. Another success to be scored.

22

WAR ENDING

❖

I n February 1918 Vernon's work brought him in touch with Mr Balfour, as he then was, for there was a question he wanted to put to him on a certain subject.[1] He came back highly delighted with one of his remarks uttered in suave and quiet tones. He had advised Vernon 'not to be disturbed by the inconvenience of an illogical situation', for they were then discussing the case of rather a well-known Russian who was a good deal in the news. It was typical of Mr Balfour to turn a phrase so precisely. He listened attentively to what was wanted, and was helpful once he was convinced.

In March Vernon went to France with General Sir George Macdonogh. They stayed at a chateau at Compiègne and later went on to Rome. There, Vernon motored out to lunch with Signor Marconi and his charming wife in their beautiful house overlooking Rome.[2] The view was quite lovely and Vernon enjoyed the visit enormously. From Rome he went on to Genoa and then to Bordighera, eventually fetching up at Marseilles. He could only stay away for a few days and returned home via Boulogne. Here dense fog delayed him for two days, a horrid waste of time, but he tried to make some contacts while he waited, much hampered by almost no visibility.

The Germans were now making great efforts with a gun called Big Bertha, which they had erected on the French coast and hoped to be able to hit Paris, and were certainly to use it against our Channel ports.[3] This gun was not a success, though it did a certain amount of damage. By the end of March things looked much better for us, for the Germans were taking some very hard knocks as well as giving them.

At home we sometimes managed to vary Vernon's heavy working day with some amusing incidents. One such I recall and still smile at. It was evening and we were just about to sit down to dinner when the doorbell rang and in walked, in full evening dress, two people I had invited to share our festive board in spite of very tight rationing! I had not warned Vernon of their arrival, for truth to tell I had forgotten all about it, and heard my maid say in amazed tones as she opened the door to our visitors, 'Oh, yes, of course you are expected.' The maid was certainly not going to let us down. It was too late to do anything but hope the dinner would be sufficient for each of us to have at least one good helping on our plates. I reflected with great relief that I had just purchased a chicken requiring all my brother-in-law's meat coupons, which he had just given me. He was on short leave from France and had quite ample a supply of these coupons. I rushed down to my long-suffering cook and told her what I had done. She looked at me rather sadly, as if I was past praying for, and said little. I returned to my guests, and joined in a good laugh over my awful forgetfulness. Our visitors suggested going off to a restaurant, but I, knowing about that wonderful chicken, nodded to Vernon, hinting that things were not as bad as he feared. Well, dinner was served, the chicken was excellent, and we ended up having a Camembert cheese in perfect condition, also just given to me by my brother-in-law. Our guests looked at Vernon in much surprise, and knowing that they had not been expected, said in ironical tones, 'Well, if this is the way you live as a rule, when most of us never see such luxuries, it is really pretty thick and will you tell us how it is done.' I really think they hardly believed us when we explained that they were sharing in our good fortune as a result of my brother-in-law's visit.

The autumn came, and still the fighting was very severe; our boys were being pushed through Sandhurst and Woolwich with alarming speed. We were so short of officers, and those boys hardly had time to get through their full course in the few months of training they were given. Our elder boy was reaching the senior classes in his school and we began to wonder whether he too would be engulfed before this horrible war ended. However our hopes of victory were showing some signs of fulfilment, though in the meanwhile the fighting seemed stiffer than ever.

Vernon went to Ireland in September to see how the work of watching, examining and clearing the people arriving at the ports was being carried out. He found all going smoothly, those in charge keenly alive to the reasons for these examinations and most anxious to collaborate with him.

I had taken our family over to my old home in the south for the holidays and Vernon was thankful when we returned safely, for the mail boat we travelled in was always in danger from submarines. She zigzagged her course across quite unharmed however, for we really thought that the Germans did not want to antagonise the Irish by making bigger efforts to hit either the mail boat or the boat crossing by long sea from Fishguard to Cork. Vernon was persuaded that it was most unlikely that they would let these two ships escape their attacks longer than it suited their plans, and was therefore not surprised to receive the news a little later that the *Leinster*, the mail boat, on the way back to Holyhead had been torpedoed with the loss of five hundred people. He knew the Germans meant to hit every ship as soon as they were satisfied that the Irish would give them no help in refuelling their submarines in certain ports. Wonderful tales had been told of their having been so assisted, but it was never proved that this had ever happened.

We were all horrified at the sinking of the *Leinster* carrying chiefly civilians, many of them women and children. One entire family whose father was a friend of Vernon's was drowned, except the mother who was amongst the saved and she, poor woman, only wished that the curious chance that rescued her had not succeeded. The Cork to Fishguard ship, the old *Inniscarra*, was torpedoed shortly after this; she was almost an institution, taking people across day in, day out. It was thought the Germans would not consider it worth their while to sink her. But things were black for them, now they were showing signs of cracking, and these sinkings seemed carried out merely for spite. It seemed to come quite suddenly, this cracking of the magnificent forces of Germany, for though, as a last horrible means of breaking our morale they had used mustard gas, we ourselves had produced something to which there could be no answer. The sudden appearance of our tanks in the field caused the maximum surprise, and the Germans had no hope of any retaliation. The secret of the tank attacks had been well guarded and the effect was devastating – just what was needed to help in bringing the war to an end. At last breaking point was reached and on November 7th the Germans asked for armistice terms. On the momentous November 11th the maroons went off in London, and this time it was to inform us that the armistice terms had been signed.

Can I describe the excitement, the relief, the joy of that morning! It was greater than any pen could tell. We rushed into the streets, the crowds gathering rapidly and surging towards Whitehall, there to rejoice madly, gladly, singing and dancing to relieve the pent-up feeling that oppressed us for so long. Nobody felt like work for a while, but that had to go on just the same, though now Vernon and everyone in his office worked with light hearts after all those long years of strain and stress. There was a victory ball at the Albert Hall in aid of Red Cross funds and to this we all went. It was a wonderful sight, and the excitement enormous, for it still seemed almost too good to be true that we had really finished with all that the war brought with it of horror and deprivation. It took some time before the food situation eased, for it had really been a very near thing, only another two or three months' food left in the country and starvation had loomed as a stark possibility in the near future. General Foch[4] and the grand old man Clemenceau[5] arrived in London on December 1st and they were given a rapturous welcome. On December 26th President Wilson arrived, and there were large crowds to greet him too.[6] Great hopes were centred on him, for if America would really take a share in solving the way to peace we dreamed of this war being one to end wars.

President Wilson went off to Paris and put before the Peace Conference his famous 'fourteen points' and his hope of lessening world tension.[7] The disillusion which followed, after our hopes had been pitched so high, was all the more intense as we gradually came to realise that Mr Wilson had not the backing from America that he expected. And now began that long road of bitter disappointment and frustration which seemed so endless. Those who could look ahead saw the danger of a second World War more dreadful than the first, looming in the distance. Vernon would speak rather gloomily of the efforts of the League of Nations and those of the League of Nations Union, for he knew only too well that the powers in Europe would not be able to fulfil the hopes centred on them. Looking back as I do now, many years after the conclusion of the Second World War, I realise how right he was when he said that not till we had passed through many bitter experiences and had grown immeasurably more mature, would it be at all possible for a League of Nations to carry out the aims set before them.

At the end of 1918 a worldwide epidemic of influenza struck us down.[8] The loss of life was appalling; the toll it took was greater than that of all the casualties in the four years of war. Vernon and all the family went down with it and we were a very sorry household just about Christmastime.

Though the war was over Vernon found little to change in the methods of work in the office. Great vigilance was required now that the vast concentrations of people organised for war were being broken up. During the anxious four years we had just been through there had been so much goodwill and eagerness to help the country in time of need, but the moment hostilities ceased the old stresses and strains and class feeling returned. It was only to be expected that those who had given up good jobs to join the defence services were worried with the fear of being unable to get them back, or to find new ones. They were impatient at the delay in being demobbed.[9] There was also the thousands of foreigners in our midst who needed very careful watching. But now the staff at MI5 could certainly relax, and some of them had the bright idea of getting up an entertainment amongst themselves, which they called the 'Hush Hush Show'.[10] It was a clever take-off of all the bosses of the various sections, rather merciless in some cases, but all taken in very good part and most amusing. Vernon was very convincingly caricatured and he was delighted with the thrusts at him, for they had got him walking with his familiar stoop and with all his tricks of manner. The show was followed by a really good dance, and the whole thing was voted a great success.

Vernon went off for a few days' fishing to Alnwick when the weather got a little warmer. It was good fun, though the trout were elusive. He had an invitation to try his luck in several of the rivers in that district, and enjoyed staying in the hotel at Alnwick that overlooked the golf course and is near the sea. It was one of his favourite places to stay. I went there with him one year, and realised why he liked it so much. My ideas on fly fishing were most elementary, though I loved trying my hand at it and Vernon would stand watching my efforts to disentangle my most erratic fly with amusement, for I would have to let him rescue me eventually. I hooked in the grass behind me or in the overhanging bushes to the left and right. The stream itself I mostly managed to avoid, however I did catch a few unwary fish, but never of any size. In spite of my want of skill, he gave me every encouragement, also a gift of a really lovely little rod, which deserved better handling than I could give. He threw out a line with such grace and skill that I found myself either in dark despair watching him, or given over to resigned admiration. It was just that I was no real use as a fisherwoman, but loved our fishing trips together, and indeed in later years a fishing holiday was what we looked forward to most of all.

On June 28th peace was actually signed in the afternoon at Versailles. One wonders now how the mistakes that were made in that peace treaty could have been avoided.

In 1919 General Sir George Macdonogh's time as Director of Military Intelligence was over, and he was succeeded by General Sir William Thwaites – also a great friend of Vernon's, who was delighted to hear of his appointment.[11] It was in that same year that Vernon thought of forming the dinner club which he called the IP.[12] What did it stand for, he was asked. 'Well,' he would laugh, 'I suppose it stands for Intelligent People!' There were to be two dinners a year and male members of his past and present staff were eligible to join. Vernon was president, the rule being that there should be only one short after-dinner speech, that of the president, for it was to be a purely friendly gathering and some special guests were to be invited each time. The first two dinners went well; there were no ladies present but I was allowed just to peep into the large dining room at the Hyde Park Hotel and see the preparations being made and enjoy the beautiful table decorations. The management took great pride in endeavouring to make these dinners the best to be had in London. I have heard it said that Vernon's short speech was most entertaining, and the few rather spicy stories he told were greeted with much merriment and applause. He had become a good speaker, for he constantly lectured to people in various branches of the services interested in intelligence, and he got the reputation of being one of the lecturers they liked best. Though when they compared notes, his audiences had to confess, that interesting though he was to listen to they had really come away with no secret information whatsoever – he was much too clever to give anything away.

Vernon felt that the time had come to begin to cut down the staff of MI5 and get back to peacetime conditions.[13] He greatly regretted saying goodbye to those who had become most efficient in his department. There were many who had given up their jobs during wartime and now had to return to them. They had most important business interests that must be attended to and they hoped that, at last, they could settle down to a peaceful existence. At that time there really was a feeling that Lloyd George's words might come true and that this was the war to end wars – so much so that boys leaving school had no desire to join the army or the navy.[14] The air force beckoned more successfully, being so full of adventure, and was now such a new branch of the fighting services. Vernon smiled when our elder boy said he thought it would be useless now to go to Sandhurst – he felt sure that there would be no more wars. His father considered it impossible to envisage a long period of peace while the world was still so little ready to accept the League of Nations as a means of settling the thorny questions facing the nations. Eventually Jim decided to try for Sandhurst, for already there was less talk of 'no more wars'.

23

STEPS BACK TO
NORMAL

❖

A very pleasant surprise awaited Vernon, for he received a message from Baron d'Erlanger saying that if he felt inclined for a visit to Paris he would be delighted to arrange that a suite of rooms at the big hotel in the Place de la Republique be put at Vernon's disposal and all expenses at the hotel paid for.[1] He was to take his wife and daughter and stay at least a fortnight. I asked in amazement why such a generous offer should have been made, and Vernon said it was in recognition of some kindness he had been able to do for the Baron and which he now wished to repay in this delightful manner. Of course we planned what could be done in that fortnight with such eagerness that even a month would not have been sufficient to carry out all we thought of. We started on June 10th and arrived at the hotel to find a most luxurious suite awaiting us and all the hotel staff ready to do all they could to please. We took tickets for the opera and how we loved that performance of Faust. Next day was a grilling hot day so we hired a car and went off to Versailles where we could get cool in the lovely gardens. The highlight of our visit was going to the Trocadero to see Madame Pavlova dance.[2] It will always remain a wonderful memory. That crowded house, the almost breathtaking beauty and grace of Pavlova's dancing, for she seemed lifted in mid-air as she swayed this way and that with her dainty feet barely tipping the floor, her whole self seemed as light as the snowflakes she was portraying. At the end of her programme came the most beautiful dance of all, 'The Death of the Swan' – her exquisite movements, especially those in the finale with its pathos and tragedy, brought tears to our eyes. Surely no one has ever danced like that before or ever will again. She seemed almost not of this earth. The audience, that vast audience, was spellbound and as she finished there was complete silence and then slowly, very slowly, the clapping began in volume till it was rapturous. We left the Trocadero still under the spell of that beautiful dancer, and never should we lose the wonder that she cast about us.

It seemed all too soon when we had to go home again. We were full of gratitude to Baron d'Erlanger for his delightful invitation that had given us such a wonderful holiday. Vernon, as a matter of fact, had been able to combine business with pleasure and had seen many of the people he had cooperated with during the war years. He still needed their help and they found their talks most useful.

Back in London he became interested in the Japan Society formed to promote interchange of thought between the Japanese and British members. Lectures were often given, dinners and social occasions were many, and when the Crown Prince Hirohito arrived on his state visit, the society played a big part in entertaining him.[3] There was hope that this visit might bring east and west together in closer sympathy. How differently the pages of history could have been written had the efforts made to bring about a better understanding between Japan and us been more successful. Our friendliness and theirs was most apparent, but the policies that Japan found difficult to square with her ideas of what was required remained unchanged.

The Japan Society continued its work and was greatly helped by the enthusiasm of one of its keenest members, Major General Sir FSG Piggott, and by Colonel John Somerville, who was the secretary for many years and gave most devoted service.[4] Both these men believed ardently that friendship and realisation of Japan's aspirations would lead to a strengthening of the bonds which could be forged to bring about real peace. Vernon became so interested that he consented to be chairman of the Japan Society for one year.

He also belonged to the China Society through which he could renew his acquaintance with many of the friends who had been so hospitable while we were in Tientsin. This society too gave very pleasant dinners and a chance of happy reunions with old friends from the Far East.

At the turn of the year 1921 the peace with Ireland was signed. Would it make much difference, we wondered? Those who carried out the negotiations certainly thought so, and Michael Collins, who was one of the Irish signatories, took a great personal risk in signing.[5] The extremists in Ireland were dead against it, but Michael Collins believed that a real peace might gradually evolve. He paid for his belief with his life – for shortly afterwards he was murdered. He had great courage and was a genuine patriot: straight thinking and straight doing. He was one of the strongest of all the leaders in the 'Irish War', as ardent nationalists called it. His death was a calamity, as was that of Kevin O'Higgins, another of those whose dealings were straight and who could be trusted to be fair.[6] He too was murdered by extremists. It took a long time for any semblance of good government to be established.

In our own home quite big changes were taking place. Our son was leaving Sandhurst, and our daughter was almost grown up and she was enjoying her social life to the full. Our younger son was still at preparatory school and seemed musical. He was allowed occasionally to play the organ in the school chapel for a service and took the hymns at breakneck pace. Later on when at Charterhouse he played the piano well, but gave all his spare time to sports for he became really good at running. At the spring sports day, when he was captain of athletics, he won the 100 yards, 220 yards and the quarter mile, beating the public-school record, and finally got the Victor Ludorum Cup. Vernon managed to go down on the day he won the cup and came back very thrilled; it really had been a most exciting day. Our daughter was now becoming quite a good singer and would have loved to take singing up as a profession. She was a pianist too, and between us we often had very enjoyable musical evenings. Vernon

151

found them a source of great pleasure and relaxation; he loved being with his family and they enjoyed it too, for he was so understanding, so quick to appreciate and so wise to counsel. There was a harmony in our home, which was entirely owing to his influence, for there was a certain serenity about him that was felt by us all. Often people who came to visit us told me that they felt this atmosphere of happiness the moment they came into the house. His children looked up to him, realising that not only was he a deeply religious man but that he practised his religion with the greatest sincerity. He was certainly their best friend and they could confide in him absolutely.

During the summer Vernon had an invitation to bring his daughter with him and join a party of friends who were to be the guests of Colonel Sir Wyndham and Lady Murray, and go with them for a trip in their steam yacht *Cecilia*.[7] They were to cruise along the coast and eventually finish up at Oban and see the games. Vernon could only spare a few days to be with them and spent an amazing time when the yacht dropped anchor in Poole Harbour and the whole party went ashore to call on Mrs van Raalte who was then the owner of Brownsea Island and lived at Sandbanks.[8] She reigned supreme in Brownsea and amused them all with the description of the feudal rights she possessed as owner, even, she said with a laugh, to pronouncing the death sentence, though she felt it might be wiser not to exercise this particular right.

On Vernon's return to London he found much to do in dealing with a spy case of considerable interest. It was an exciting chase, this time leading to a town near Edinburgh. The suspect had very cleverly covered up his tracks and seemed completely innocent. But Vernon felt sure that the evidence he required before this man could be arrested was there somewhere, and refused to give up the search. He knew he had booked a passage and meant to leave the country at once – there was no time to lose – but everything had been tried and so far failure. He decided to come himself and search, not a trace of anything incriminating, yet he felt positive that it was there concealed somewhere. Vernon looked once more at this notebook … absolutely nothing. In the many letters, nothing either. What was to be done? The sun was shining very brightly in at the window where Vernon was standing holding up the notebook to the light and examining it page by page, when suddenly he detected a slight extra thickness in one of the pages and discovered that two of them were cunningly stuck together. On very delicately separating them, he found what he was looking for – a message written in code and invisible ink! Success, yes but could he get the spy arrested in time, for the hour at which his ship was to sail was fast approaching. It was a Sunday and nothing could be done without the warrant from the local provost. Vernon hurriedly arrived at the provost's house, and was told that he was in bed and could not be disturbed. Vernon sent an urgent request for him to come downstairs, but was again informed that the provost was feeling ill and could not come. A message, this time in really forceful language, was sent up, for time was slipping away and no move as yet from the provost. At last a very pale, dishevelled man appeared, saying very ruefully, for he had dined well on the previous night, 'I feel awful sick.' He certainly looked it. Risking what might happen at any moment, Vernon got him to sign the necessary warrant which was served just in the nick of time. The spy was arrested and his activities were cut short, for he was given quite a long term of imprisonment.

Vernon was now working out completely new methods of countering enemy efforts to obtain secret information. He felt certain that enemy agents would employ different techniques and the old ones scrapped. Believing so little in the efficacy of the League of Nations he considered it too soon to expect much change in the policies of the great powers which alone could make it possible for the ideals of the League of Nations to bear fruit. Through the years between the two wars he continued to work out the methods that would enable him and his most able staff to counter the activities of potential enemies.

But here is another instance of the older methods of German agents in this country. During the First World War they were using neutrals such as Brazilians, Swedes, Uruguayans, Peruvians – all of them actuated by various motives, mostly for money but very seldom from any affection for Germany. One such, a so-called purchaser of large quantities of Norwegian tinned fish, presented himself when questioned as a perfectly innocent commercial traveller. But it was not the season for this tinned fish to be on the market.[9] So he was watched, and soon his various interested inquiries in military centres and his approaches to known persons of doubtful reliability amongst the local naturalised Germans led to his arrest. Incriminating papers were found on him and he was found guilty of spying. Such efforts would be far too crude when the much more intricate and complicated plots to evade our counter-espionage would be used effectively through radar, aeroplanes at great heights and at high speed, scientific methods of all sorts, and the unblushing use of diplomatic bags. These methods would immensely increase our difficulties and a completely different system would be necessary. Time would show, Vernon was convinced of that.

At the War Office the Director of Military Intelligence was Major General Sir Jock Burnett-Stuart, who had succeeded Major General Sir William Thwaites.[10] He was a good friend of Vernon's; they had known each other many years and his appointment was most welcome to him. He knew he would help with enthusiasm.

In 1923 Vernon joined the British Institute of International Affairs, beautifully housed in St James's Square. It was intended for those who wished to study the internal affairs of both western and eastern nations. There was an excellent library and there were to be frequent lectures by men of note, to further their studies. As a member, Vernon could take me with him to hear some of the lectures, many of them most remarkable. Amongst others, we were lectured to by Mahatma Ghandi, who spoke eloquently. As he concluded, several of his own countrymen got up to refute some of his remarks, and to put questions to him that he found difficult to answer. They too were eloquent, but much more realistic than Ghandi, who remained perfectly calm and dignified and replied to his questioners with not a trace of irritation at their disagreement. It was most impressive. Another fascinating lecture was given by Dr Benes of Czechoslovakia.[11] We felt that if it were possible for his hope to be fulfilled, his country could go forward peacefully and with confidence. He was to have a rude awakening!

At that time we ourselves were in the midst of a political turmoil, for Mr Baldwin had put forward a tariff reform policy and had a very strong faction against him at the polls when a general election took place at the end of the year.[12] The tariff reform policy, as a rallying cry, had completely failed and his defeat gave the socialists their first chance of governing. They could hardly be said to be in power, but they were in the saddle, and Ramsay MacDonald had his chance.[13] That was in December.

Early the following year Vernon returned home with a copy of the *News of the World*. This newspaper had printed columns of information about him and his work, giving details of interesting cases, some true enough and some very much off the mark. They had noticed that Vernon and his next senior officer had appeared in the *Gazette* as no longer on active service, and considered that they could now disregard all appeals for silence in matters dealing with his work in MI5. They did not know that in his case, being listed as no longer on active service meant nothing more than still further work, even more unobtrusively done than before. We had a good laugh over the columns of print telling about the sensational cases brought to book previous to and during the 1914 war, and particularly over a very fierce-looking photograph of Vernon which made him look thoroughly ruthless. Subsequently, no more news of him appeared in the papers and he was satisfied that he was now well camouflaged.

Things were not going very smoothly for the Labour government and it was not long before we were once more facing a general election, for they had been defeated on a vote of censure dealing with a subject that had caused disquiet in the country. I did a certain amount of canvassing, accompanied by a very witty Irishwoman. We compared notes of our experiences and her tale, told with a rich Irish brogue, was the best I heard. She said she had been trying to persuade a woman to use her vote, but was receiving no encouragement, when the woman suddenly said, 'If I vote at all, I will vote communist,' with the accent on the second syllable, 'for I am a good communicant.' After that my friend gave up! In the evenings I related some of our experiences to Vernon who thought the communicant story good enough for *Punch*, but some of the others he thought most pathetic, for it was plain that many of the people we had talked to considered the government responsible for most of their ills. When the Conservatives came in with their sweeping victory great things were expected of them. But it was no easy task to steer the ship of state through very troubled waters, for restlessness and insecurity made tempers high and situations difficult.

24

VISIT TO SOUTH AFRICA

❧

E arly in 1925 Vernon and I celebrated our silver wedding anniversary – a big family affair ending up with a dance. My mother, who had come over from Ireland, made a most telling little speech, and was the success of the evening. A few days afterwards, Vernon brought a very interesting guest to dinner. He had been in prison in Russia during the first revolution. The stories he told of what the prisoners had to go through baffled description; gently nurtured men and women herded together in horrible prisons, starved and tortured, the sick left to die untended; some of the tales were too painful to listen to. He said that he, being an Englishman, was better treated than the rest. He could speak Russian fluently and lost no opportunity to impress the guards and warders with the fact that dreadful things could happen to them if those in power in England should hear that they had tortured him. Of course it was an empty threat, but it actually did impress the guards, and though they starved him they did not torture him. He said that it was curious that after many months of starvation he no longer wanted a decent meal. When he finally got away and stood on the platform awaiting the train that was to take him to the border he saw a man with a large basket of tomatoes and he eagerly asked if he could buy some. 'Of course,' said the man, and gave him a few – but as soon as he had tasted one and got through half he threw it away, quite unable to finish it – no desire whatever to eat his fill. He had many adventures that might have led to his being imprisoned again, but he did at last get away and returned to England.

In the Second World War prisoners were treated much worse, not only by the Russians but also by the Germans, who harnessed science to aid them in the horrible tortures they thought out to break the spirit of their prisoners. Now that some years have passed since these things happened we once more hopefully look forward to a future which will not tolerate such treatment. But we still wait.

In 1926 the unrest in England came to a head in the general strike.[1] Unemployment, insecurity and difficulties of all sorts culminated in a complete stoppage of all work, even in the most essential means of feeding our great towns. It was tackled without any of the consequences that might have arisen – no bloodshed or even rioting. Volunteers came forward to take the place of the workers while they waited for their grievances to be heard, and as far as our experiences here in London went, the provision of food went forward most efficiently. Transport was successfully dealt with and trains were running, telephone exchanges were manned, newspapers in single sheets were printed, wireless was used to the utmost to direct our movements, and in a very short time we were back to normal and the workers returned. But the coal strike continued for it was only too true that the miners were in great distress, and so little could be done for them.

There was a most interesting musical event that summer, for the Russian Opera came to Covent Garden and with them came Chaliapine, the great bass singer. We went off to hear him; Vernon loved Russian music and had heard so much of it when he was in Moscow. Besides the Russians we also had the great German singers Lotte Lehmann, Frida Leider and Elisabeth Schumann, and the famous conductor Bruno Walter gave us the most brilliant season at Covent Garden. Major Goldman, a great friend of Vernon's, had asked us down to his house at Beaulieu for the weekend to meet some of these singers. Our daughter, who was studying singing and had a really good lyrical soprano voice, was to come with us. In the evening, after a day of sailing, for Major Goldman's family were keen yachtsmen, Lotte Lehmann and Elisabeth Schumann sang to us accompanied by Bruno Walter and gave us a musical treat beyond compare. They were delightful guests, so gay and full of enthusiasm, and on our return to London our daughter let no occasion pass without going to the stage door of the opera house or to the green rooms in the concert hall when there was a chance of meeting them.

One morning Vernon went off very early to fulfil an engagement to breakfast with the Prime Minister, Mr Stanley Baldwin. He was taken all over Chequers where he saw much of interest; among other things, Baldwin showed him the death mask of Oliver Cromwell, impressive, and showing off his very fine head. Vernon was working very hard at that time and many 'birds', as he sometimes called them, were falling into the net. He seldom spoke of them – an initial here and there in his diary gave us a clue to what he was dealing with.

It was a welcome break when he could spend a weekend in the country, and I remember one that pleased us both greatly. We went to stay with General and Mrs Hare at Norwich, who were the most charming host and hostess. They drove us out to see Colonel and Mrs Bulwer, old friends of Vernon's. They lived in one of those lovely old gabled houses in their park-like settings that are the charm of Norfolk. The Bulwers were great collectors of antiques and had in their possession a large scale-model of a doll's house of a very early period and handed down to them from generations earlier. This doll's house contained miniature furniture of beautiful finish, also small period dolls, in fact models of everything required in a great house of two hundred years ago, and all in a state of wonderful preservation. They also had quite a famous collection of teapots, of every shape and size, both antique and modern. Queen Mary had been over to see it, and shortly before we were there she had sent them two very special teapots, with a message that she hoped they had not already got two like them. These teapots were arranged on tiers of shelves, pyramid shaped, so that every teapot could be handled, and I shuddered to think of the dusting of all these precious things. Mrs Bulwer said she undertook that task and would leave it to no one else.

Later on that year Vernon came in for a small legacy and we wondered whether to invest it, or to enjoy it to the full and spend it straight away. Vernon had an invitation from Admiral Sir Maurice Fitzmaurice to combine work with pleasure and come and stay at Admiralty House, Simonstown, where Sir Maurice was Commander-in-Chief.[2] As the Admiral had kindly extended his invitation to include both our daughter and me we decided to use the legacy and all go off together. It was late October when we started and we reckoned on arriving just when the spring would be beginning in November; we hoped for really warm weather. It was a very pleasant voyage; as usual the heat was terrific passing Cape Verde, but as we travelled further south it became quite cold, and on reaching Cape Town we found it was snowing, and Table Mountain was covered with a deep black cloud. This was a disappointment, but friends meeting us at the quayside assured us that this was a very rare occurrence.

The Admiral's flag lieutenant met us and motored us to Simonstown – a lovely drive giving us some idea of the beauty of the Cape in spite of the wind and rain. The Admiral made us very welcome and we soon felt at home in that charming house with its bougainvillea creeper, red and purple, climbing up the walls, and its garden full of flowers of glowing colours. Sir Maurice motored us to see many famous houses with their large estates, these mostly growing vines up the hillsides. The houses themselves were built in Old Dutch style, gabled and with stoops or verandahs, where long easy chairs invited you to sit and admire the beautiful countryside. The weather had now much improved and though cold it was very dry. What struck us most was the hard bright blue of the almost cloudless sky, the blue and emerald of the sea, and the deep purple of the mountain ranges in the far distance. The view from Admiralty House was particularly beautiful, and wherever we went we were enchanted by the views of sea and land, and only wished we could stay many weeks to get to know the Cape. We spent a fortnight at Simonstown and then, after regretfully saying goodbye to our host, we went off to a hotel at St James's Bay, which we made our headquarters. From there we could pay visits to friends both Dutch and English who had asked us and so get a glimpse of their home life. Vernon had a certain amount of work to do and this all fitted in well. There was much talk about the colour question, which was even then uppermost in people's minds. Also we felt a strong feeling of unrest, for politics were playing a large part in everyone's lives. Vernon met General Smuts who was a great power in the land, and as long as his hand was at the helm people felt that things would go smoothly.[3] But what of the future? Many books were being written and eagerly read on the burning questions of the day. There was much to think about and Vernon had learnt a great deal – it would be useful when he got home and back to work.

It was Christmastime when we arrived in London, after a voyage calm and warm, though it was both stormy and very cold in the Gulf of Lyons. We had very little time to make the usual preparations and to send out the hundreds of Christmas cards that Vernon's large connections at home and abroad called for. The annual Christmas card that his office sent out was always a special feature, and occasionally these cards illustrated very wittily what MI5 stood for.

In February our elder son gave some anxious moments when he suddenly turned up at home after an accident during a hunt with the East Kent Foxhounds, for he was badly concussed. He had a very favourite horse which he felt certain would win one of the races at a Point-to-Point event two or three days later, and intended to ride him though still suffering from concussion. His military doctor persuaded him to consult a London specialist before going in for the race, and Jim had therefore arrived home but was fully determined to ride whatever the specialist might say. He duly went to see the specialist who was rather cryptic: 'Yes you may ride, but you won't be alive after the race, so you can decide for yourself.'

It was a bitter disappointment, and he contemplated disregarding the specialist's advice. However after much persuasion and some straight talking by Vernon he decided to let a brother officer ride his horse for him. The horse won easily which was some satisfaction. Later on, after he had fully recovered, he went over to Ireland and stayed with an old friend of Vernon's, Colonel George Stacpoole, who had some of the best horses in Ireland and whose fame in the hunting field was second to none.[4] Also he had won the Grand Military two years running. We spent the best leave he had ever had in Limerick, hosted by George Stacpoole and hunting five days a week.

In the autumn of that year Vernon decided to get a good rest when his leave became due, and take our two sons and me on a cruise to the Dalmatian Coast. We enjoyed that greatly and were most interested when we reached Spalatto in going to see Diocletian's Palace, where we were surprised to find the familiar designs of the Adam brothers in the interior decorations of the palace. We had not realised till then that the Adam brothers had taken many of their ideas from sketches they had made in the palace. At Ragusa, or Dubrovnik as it is now called, we had to brush up on our history, for the enormous walls and fortifications of that picturesque town recalled many a tale of desperate fighting and heroic deeds in bygone days. In the evening we sat under the trees on the large quay and listened to a gaily uniformed band which delighted us with its sparkling music, reminiscent of Rossini's operas. Returning to our ship we cruised towards Rhodes, where we saw the magnificent building of the Knights of St John. The spirit of the crusaders seemed still to pervade these medieval halls and churches. We wished we could have spent some time in Rhodes to give us a chance of seeing all the buildings of such historic interest, but that was the one drawback of a cruise such as this; we had to move on and keep strictly to dates in our floating hotel, however great was our desire to stay on anywhere.

When we returned home we were soon involved in a house move which meant our leaving Camden Hill for Evelyn Gardens. We needed a large house: ours had become too cramped, especially as my mother had decided to give up our home in Ireland and come to live with us in London, for a time anyway. We worked hard to be ready by Christmas and were able to have all the family parties. Vernon, in particular, liked the new house, and found Evelyn Gardens more central than living on Campden Hill.

In the following year General Smuts came to visit England for a few weeks, making London his headquarters. He lectured at the Bureau of International Affairs, his subject being the British Empire and the League of Nations. We went to hear him. He was a most persuasive speaker; his wide authority and foreseeing mind, and his sturdy idealism, fired us all with enthusiasm. Had his ideas been brought to fruition the political situation in South Africa would have developed very differently, but the Second World War changed everything and his hopes were not fulfilled.

After our daughter's wedding in June Vernon had to go to Cairo and took me with him. We stayed there with great friends, Colonel Charles Congreve and his wife. Vernon was able to carry out the work he had planned, and we had time to do some sightseeing which we much enjoyed. Jim, our elder son, was stationed with his regiment in the citadel barracks and we saw much of him. Brigadier Dobbie, who later became so famous during the defence of Malta, was an old friend of Vernon's and was in Cairo at the time. He was a most remarkable man, and those who knew him were not surprised that he was able to inspire the people of Malta with his courage and confidence when the test came during the war.

The Congreves arranged several expeditions for us to visit the most historic places in and around Cairo. We were deeply impressed by the Step Pyramid at Sakara, surely one of the most wonderful buildings in the world. The Tutankhamun treasures in the museum fascinated us, also the many beautiful mosques, and we were taken to see a religious ceremony, a dance of the dervishes, which was very impressive.

Vernon had to return after about a fortnight and once more found work so much on the increase that he had to enlarge his staff considerably. At the time there was much publicity in the papers regarding the Baillie-Stewart case.[5] He was a young officer who had such a low standard of loyalty that he played into the hands of those plotting to damage his own country. When it was found out, he had to suffer the punishment that brought with it disgrace and much bitterness to his family, for his father, who was a fine old soldier, felt it terribly. It was one of those rare cases of a British officer letting down his country; always it had been our proud boast that this could not happen here.

In Germany things were beginning to look very questionable. It was quite understandable that Adolf Hitler was making a great bid to lead Germany back to her place as a great power and to give her people the self-esteem which they had largely lost. That was indeed entirely laudable, but would it stop there? Such people as Sir Robert Vansittart, as he then was, warned us repeatedly not to believe that Hitler's zeal for efficiency and training was simply a plan for the betterment of Germany and had no sinister significance. Vernon was persuaded that Germany would take the first opportunity for aggression the moment she felt strong enough. Mussolini was also worth watching though he had not, as yet, shown his hand. His intentions however, were exceedingly suspect.

At home things were looking pretty gloomy, for the unemployment situation was desperate and hunger marchers approached London. It was an intensely difficult situation to deal with for though the sympathy for so much unemployment was great, the plans to relieve it were utterly inadequate. Fascists too were stirring up still more trouble and making a bid for power. Discontent was general, fanned by the flames lit by people of various convictions, for socialists, communists and fascists, the tub-thumping orators in places like Hyde Park, had much fertile ground to work on. They certainly made full use of it, which increased the sense of distress and discontent among the people.

In 1935 came Hitler's defiance of the Versailles Treaty and the introduction of conscription in Germany. 'Straws in the wind,' wrote Vernon in his diary, for things were developing quickly now that Hitler was growing less cautious.

In May of that year we celebrated the Silver Jubilee of King George V and Queen Mary; this was a great occasion, the streets were packed with rejoicing crowds, and the King and Queen received a great ovation. There was such real affection in evidence that day; everyone wished them joy and was so glad to see the King restored to health after his recent grave illness. Vernon and I were watching the royal procession from the Naval & Military Club in Piccadilly and felt the surge of welcome given by the enormous crowds to be quite unusually sincere and enthusiastic. The royal couple could not fail to realise how very dear they had become to us all.

Later in the year there was the Naval Review, which was an inspiring sight. Vernon and I had been asked to be guests of the Admiralty on board the ship chartered by them for the benefit of the many hundreds of privileged people who were to spend two days of a wonderful holiday watching the review. Our fellow guests were most interesting for they came from many walks of life and from different parts of the world. The review ended with a brilliant display of fireworks and we went back to London the next day feeling very proud of our fleet.

Our rejoicing could not last long, for rumours of war were growing louder. As autumn drew near we heard the sabre-rattling Mussolini to declare war on Abyssinia, for he was determined to enlarge the Italian possessions in North Africa. Where would it all lead to? Vernon had no doubts as to the eventual results of what both Mussolini and Hitler were planning.

In December, our younger son John's marriage took place at Chelsea Old Church.[6] Both he and his bride were very young, and looked out bravely at the future – rumours of war did not in the least impress them. They felt sure that there was every reason why Hitler should need peace to enable him to carry out his ideas for strengthening Germany and restoring her position of greatness in Europe. They decided to come and live in London and though this was very pleasant for us, Vernon rather doubted the wisdom of their taking on the lease of a house.

25

GEORGE VI COMES TO THE THRONE

❧

I t was in a very troubled world that Edward VIII was called upon to become our king and emperor.[1] Shortly after his coming to the throne there was a curious incident. The King was presenting colours to the guards, when a man stepped out from among the crowds looking on and threatened him with a revolver. I remember most distinctly on that occasion that the King remained perfectly calm, not taking the slightest notice of this man. The assailant, called McMahon, was arrested and sent for trial; he stated that he had only meant to alarm the King.[2] If that was his motive it had completely failed.

The daily papers were now constantly filled with reports of Hitler's activities and speeches, whipping up enthusiasm among his followers. Some friends of Vernon's, newly arrived from Germany, gave him graphic descriptions of what they had seen and heard at meetings in Nuremberg where Hitler was greeted with particular fervour. These friends had brought back newspapers with many illustrations of young men carrying spades over their shoulders, marching and countermarching in almost regimental formation. They carried banners with inflammatory slogans, their faces expressing most unhealthy exaltation. These friends of Vernon's thought Hitler was simply aiming at lifting the Germans out of the despondency they had been in since 1918; they could see no danger in the wild enthusiasm that greeted Hitler everywhere. Vernon and I constantly listened on the wireless to the torrent of words with which Hitler addressed those young men – it seemed a systematic working up to a purpose which was clear enough but which such admirers as those friends of ours only regarded as being directed to rightful and peaceful resuscitation of the German people. A handshake with Hitler, which several of them had welcomed, seemed to them a sign of great friendliness for the British, for Hitler's meetings with foreigners were certainly a clever move on his part. But it was obvious by this time that his speeches were purely incitement to a war of revenge. It was just a case of watching and waiting for the moment that he would decide to move. All those with inside information were apprehensive as to what form that action would take.

Our country was now going through a period of great tension, and as we reached its climax it became evident that King Edward VIII wished to abdicate. The situation was intensely delicate and difficult; the King's subjects felt the greatest sympathy for him, but most of them were convinced that, under the circumstances, there was no other course open to him than to abdicate, which would enable him to marry the woman of his choice. When his brother came to the throne we looked to him as a man worthy of the great traditions which he must uphold, and which, as time went on, we saw him enhance with ever-growing confidence. He soon won not only the admiration of his people but also their very real affection.

In May 1937 preparations for his coronation were in full swing. The decorations in streets and houses were quite lovely. We hoped for a fine day and May 12th did not disappoint us. The dense crowds lining the streets were tense with excitement when the royal procession appeared. They arrived at the abbey and the King and Queen with the little Princesses stepped into the annex prepared for their reception. Our elder son was one of the ushers and as the royal party came in little Princess Margaret slipped her hand into his and said, 'What do we do now?' She was enchanting as she looked up at him with her bright smile.

Soon the King and Queen were ready to move into the abbey and that beautiful coronation service began. It was deeply moving, a wonderful privilege to be present. Vernon and I were guests of Sir Philip Game, then Commissioner of Police, and we had a very fine view of the royal procession from his rooms at Scotland Yard.[3] Everyone was in high spirits, for much good was expected of the King.

On May 20th we went to see the Naval Review at Spithead. It was a fine day, with a stiff breeze blowing, and on board the *Strathmore*, the P&O ship in which the Admiralty accommodated their guests, we had a wonderful view of the fleet. We noted with much amusement the eagerness with which the German naval attaché, one of the many guests on board, rattled off at great speed every detail of size, speed, guns and other information of as many ships as he could point out to the high-ranking German naval officer who had come specially to be present at the review. The flow of words was so rapid that the high-ranking officer gave up in despair trying to follow the complicated information supplied to him and he quietly walked away, leaving a rather deflated enthusiast standing. As soon as it was dark that evening the fleet was illuminated and the searchlights turned on; they made an intricate pattern in the sky with their shafts of light weaving this way and that. Soon the fireworks began – a fine show, accompanied by the acclamation of the crowds on shore whenever something specially beautiful was displayed. It was all most enjoyable, and indeed quite unforgettable, for never again would the British Navy have such a vast array of ships assembled at Spithead. Things were changing so rapidly, our needs for defence and offence would have to change too, and many of our big ships would no longer be required.

In the following month Vernon and I were invited to stay with General Sir Maurice Taylor and his wife at Aldershot to see the Tattoo.[4] It took place on a lovely summer's night. We were staying at one of the official houses, and our host and hostess had also invited Sir Walford Davies, the famous musician, and his wife to be their guests.[5] To hear Sir Walford at the piano after we had returned from the Tattoo was delightful, for he played with great artistic insight, especially some of our simplest folk songs; his rendering of them was given with such evident love of their beauty. Vernon, who was so musical, listened quite entranced and could have remained all night by the piano if we could have persuaded Sir Walford to continue. Vernon was quite a good pianist himself but never had time to keep it going.

In August of that year Vernon and I went for a few days' fishing near Alnwick. He had little success for the fish were not rising and the water too low, so we went off for a short motor tour to visit Hadrian's Wall and the Roman Camps, still in such a remarkably good state of preservation. Our next destination was Boroughbridge, and from there we motored to the Moors near Whitby and Scarborough. Whitby used to be such a charming old-world little town, now modernised to its detriment. It is very overcrowded and has all that attracts seaside holidaymakers: noise, bustle, dancing halls, shooting galleries, no doubt bringing prosperity to the town. At one time Whitby was a real artist's resort, with its picturesque fisherman's cottages built at all angles up the steep cliff side and the ruins of the old abbey overlooking the town. The shelling of the German submarines in the 1914 war destroyed most of what was left of the abbey's lovely east window. Whitby, with all its improvements, had lost all its charm; only hustle and noise and the evident quick turnover of money had taken the place of all that was attractive twenty years earlier.

On the following Sunday we motored to York to see the Minster, and sat close to the famous Seven Sisters Window, surely one of the most beautiful to be found anywhere. We listened to the music in that superb setting, and to the singing of the famous choir, glad to forget for the moment the stress and strain of the times we lived in. Curious the way one had a sense of foreboding all through those years, the longing for peace was so great, yet the sense of unrest and frustration even greater. Hearing Vernon's comments on the many disturbing events in Germany and in other countries, not only in Europe, I was left in no doubt as to the probabilities of a war horrible to contemplate. Our children were too young to be involved in the First World War, but what of the next? Our two sons would certainly be fighting in that one. It would take all the nation had to give to fight it successfully, but we knew it would be our dauntless spirit that would take us to the top. Outwardly everything was going on just as usual. Christmas came with its gaieties, and the New Year 1938 was greeted with every sign of merriment. If we felt foreboding it was never apparent, and what there was to enjoy, we certainly enjoyed to the full.

Vernon had many consultations with the DMI, Major General Sir William Bartholomew – there were always difficulties to be solved.[6] Subjects such as Percy Glading and Albert Williams were brought to trial and given terms of imprisonment.[7] These were just some of the smaller fry that were being netted. It was anxious work, so much depended on keeping well in front of any new schemes that might be launched by those interested in defeating our watchfulness.

Hitler had now marched his troops into Austria; the *Anschluss* was complete. Ribbentrop, his ambassador, played his cards here with great assurance and was a social success. Though he failed to appreciate that we as a nation were likely to oppose Hitler's designs, and his reassuring advice to him was based on a complete misapprehension of our reactions.[8]

Anthony Eden resigned his post in the government and made it only too evident that there was wide dissatisfaction with the drift that he considered was going on in parliament.[9] He felt that Neville Chamberlain's fervent hope that common sense would prevail and deter Hitler from carrying out his plans was quite unrealistic. We were now approaching summer. May Day passed off quietly at Hyde Park; many had feared there might be disturbances but no doubt the feeling of apprehension of what might lie before us kept the agitators quiet.

In the autumn Vernon accepted an invitation from Sir Russell Scott and his wife to go and stay with them in their new house near Forres.[10] Sir Russell had only just retired from his post as head of the Home Office where Vernon had been in constant touch with him. I was also invited, and we were to bring our fishing rods, for the Findhorn and Spey rivers were not far away. We enjoyed that holiday even more than usual. It was so peaceful, and the country all around us was beautiful. We returned in time to go to one of the afternoon tea parties at Buckingham Palace, which was really delightful. There was a charming informality about them; the King and Queen moving amongst us and making each one feel so welcome. We were in the Long Gallery and could enjoy to the full the pictures in that famous collection. Time seemed to fly as we looked first at one masterpiece, then another, and we could hardly tear ourselves away when we had to leave.

By September things were looking so threatening in Europe that we started definite preparations in case war should break out. The socialists were still pacifically inclined, and Neville Chamberlain was playing for time. Vernon was very uneasy and wondered how much longer the indecision would last. I expect that the years 1933–1939 will be written up in history with many divergent opinions, but all will agree that we started much too late to make ready for a war which was to prove so terrible and so long drawn out. In his diary Vernon put three words: 'things look blacker' – expressive enough of what was felt at the time, with so little being done towards defence, and still less of offence. Vernon now decided to move part of his office staff to a less vulnerable place than they then occupied, leaving a larger nucleus in London itself. The last IP dinner had been given – a particularly brilliant one. Perhaps some of the guests felt that it might well be the final one, which indeed it proved to be for it was never revived after the war.

Neville Chamberlain now made his dramatic decision to fly over to Berchtesgaden to meet Hitler himself. He felt certain that a straight talk with him would have beneficial consequences, and he came back with what he considered was an undertaking by Hitler not to wage war against us. He returned to be given a rapturous welcome by the crowds who thought that Hitler's assurances could be taken at their face value. But many people were most apprehensive of Hitler's peaceful protestations; they feared they might slow down the preparations we were making to fight a war they felt would most certainly be launched against us.

A rather strange cocktail party was given by the German military attaché, while all this tension was growing. Vernon and I were invited.

It was a large party, people of many nationalities were present and all the time there was a sense of malaise, which seemed to grow more intense as the evening wore on – there was a sort of forced gaiety very apparent. A look of strain and dislike on the face of our host did not tend to improve matters, and even the very servants, all Germans, wore most forbidding expressions. Time dragged on, and at last Vernon thought we could leave, and thankfully we said goodbye to our host, whose veneer of social politeness barely covered up very evident hostility. A few days later, a similar cocktail party was given by the Japanese military attaché. This was not nearly so strained, and our host was as friendly as such an occasion warranted.

As Christmas approached the uneasiness in the country grew stronger, and we wondered how much longer we should be allowed to live in peace. Restlessness and uncertainty crept into everything. We could not relax; there was a feeling that we were watching a volcano, and expected a violent eruption at any moment.

The year 1939 started well; it was cold with a good deal of snow to make it more like Christmas. We managed to have quite a festive time, and even had Christmas trees to entertain the many people who were working in Vernon's office, and in the offices of those whose work was carried out in the same building. January and February passed quietly enough, but by March Hitler was paving the way for the annexation of Czechoslovakia, and had taken it over completely by the middle of the month.

He was persecuting the Jews, who were being hounded out of Germany and many were taking refuge over here. One, a very gifted violinist, tried hard to stay in England with his artist wife, and asked to be allowed to take up concert playing and teaching. But he had no success; it was made so impossible for him to stay by those interested only in keeping what work there was for our own musicians. He and his wife managed to get to America, where they quickly got employment and were given a warm welcome. The same thing happened to many famous doctors and surgeons who applied to be allowed to work in our hospitals – there were too many difficulties to be overcome and they too went to America where they at once found work.

The stories we heard about the treatment of Jews in Germany were almost unbelievable. Vernon had a letter from an eye witness describing how bands of youths were marched through the streets and sent into Jewish houses, where they smashed up everything they could lay their hands on: furniture, china, pictures, household goods of all sorts. At the sound of a whistle, the youths would march out of the houses, and a second batch of youths would move in to complete the wreckage, and destroy as much of the home itself as they could. Many Germans felt so disgusted that they asked the Jews into their homes to give them meals and try to help them. Vernon's correspondent, who was just a visitor spending a few weeks' holiday in Germany, said that what struck her so very unpleasantly was the look on the faces of the youths that were marched into these houses; their eyes looked half drugged, almost as if they were hypnotised. She realised it would be safer not to post her letter locally, for it might never reach Vernon, so she waited to post it in Belgium. Constant reports came in of similar events taking place all over Germany; they had become quite usual by this time and were just all in the day's work. It seemed hardly credible that this was only a very mild forerunner of what the Jews were to go through later.

26

PREPARATION FOR A
SECOND WORLD WAR

❧

V ernon was, again, greatly enlarging his staff and personnel to
be ready to meet any emergency.[1] He had a very wonderful
team to drive, they were all enthusiastic helpers. Outwardly
everything was going on as usual, for there was still hope that we might
be saved from war, though every day these hopes grew fainter. The King
and Queen were now to go to Canada on a royal visit. Vernon went down
to Portsmouth to meet those who were making the arrangements for
their journey. Their Majesties were to embark the next day, and everyone
wished them a very successful visit. We were just beginning to know the
King better and, as the years went on, he was to possess his people's
affection in most abundant measure.

Returning to London, Vernon found himself absorbed in many
new defence activities, and the field of his work continued to widen.
The Territorial Army was being mobilised in somewhat desultory
fashion, and our second son joined up in the Surrey Yeomanry. He
was given a certain amount of training, a fortnight at a time, but he
knew very little of soldiering and there seemed little opportunity to
learn. We hoped devoutly that he would get some really hard training
before the Yeomanry was called up for service, for it certainly was
most necessary.

In the spring our elder son got married and he and his wife took a flat not very far away from us, and we saw much of them. They were not left in any doubt as to what Vernon thought of the chances of peace. Summer came, and with it some very hot weather; Vernon got a few days off and went fishing near a little inn he had heard of near Launceston. On the way down we spent a couple of days at Crewkerne where our friends Sir Alexander and Lady Gibbons had a charming house and most lovely garden. They drove us to see Ford Abbey, a building of rare beauty and historical interest. It was pleasant to find this house still lived in by the family who own it. It has not shared the fate of so many of our beautiful English homes which have been left deserted, of necessity, by the old families owning them, for heavy taxation has made it impossible for them to continue to live there.

When we reached our little hotel at Wisley Down Vernon found the fishing was no good at all. But some of our fellow guests interested him – a young officer who was there with his father, a retired military man, talked of a possible war in a peculiarly detached and philosophical manner. He had every intention of fighting for his country when the time came but he was very critical of all wars, and genuinely apprehensive of the consequences of the terrible war that might have to be waged against Hitler. He was convinced that it was not the way to solve the problems that Hitler confronted us with. Vernon listened to his opinions, but asked how he proposed to deal with a dictator who could see no other way of satisfying his greed for power than by using force to the utmost. He answered warily, showing clearly that, in spite of what Hitler was successfully carrying out, he still felt that fighting him was not the answer. He left us feeling that there must be many young men who thought as he did, and would fight in the war without being persuaded that it was right to do so. There would be the spirit of adventure and, of course, loyalty to King and country, but in many cases the spirit would be lacking that made war the glorious thing that upheld most fighting men.

Returning to London we heard that Vernon's secretary, Miss Esme Barton, was to be married to the well-known correspondent George

Steer, who was to go out east shortly after his wedding.[2] Sir Sydney Barton, Esme's father, had been our ambassador in Abyssinia till he had to leave in the face of Mussolini's invading army. The wedding took place in the Savoy Chapel where the guest of honour was the Emperor Haile Selassie himself, then an exile from his country.[3] He stood at the far end of the little chapel, a picturesque figure who greeted the bride with utmost grace and dignity though his face wore a look of ineffable sadness. He was to experience many years of waiting before he could return to his own country, and this he bore with great courage, earning the respect of all who came in contact with him.

Sir Sydney Barton had lived in China for many years and while in Hong Kong had known Chiang Kai-shek before he had become famous.[4] He was then a strong, direct, incorruptible Chinaman, a fact that later made him the venerated leader of his nation. What eventually took place to cause Chiang to lose that leadership? He certainly had very big ideals for his country, and I doubt that we shall ever really know why it all went wrong.

Vernon regretfully said goodbye to his secretary, now Mrs Steer, but wished her much luck. It was tragic that her husband, so soon after going to report on the situation in the East, and fearlessly undertaking most daring tasks, should meet his death quite early in the war.

The month of July was to see the end of the London season; it was the last for a very long time. Such eventful years lay ahead of us, though in July we still hoped that something would prevent war being declared. We did, successfully, push ahead with our preparations, many of them made in feverish haste, for we realised that there was little or nothing to fall back upon were it necessary to equip very large forces to be sent abroad. One officer looked ruefully at Vernon and said, 'I'd rather be sent to fight with a gun in my hand than with a stick'.

In Vernon's office work was pouring in.[5] I asked little, and was told little. But later I heard about the activities of four enemy agents who were apprehended having landed in fishing smacks.[6] They landed in pairs, and had maps, codes and small portable wireless sets. They had also brought enough tinned food, bread and brandy to last at least a couple of weeks. Their instructions were to sleep out, but to find out all they could about our coast defences, types and numbers of guns and of troops by walking around during the daytime. They were to have prearranged hours during which they would transmit whatever information they had been able to collect, through their wireless sets. When these men were caught and questioned it was interesting to learn that the invasion of England had been seriously considered, and that the food supply of these agents was to last the fortnight that the Germans thought would elapse before their invading armies could be landed and would march on London. These enemy agents stood their trial and three of them were convicted, the fourth one having convinced his interrogators that he had been forced to undertake a job he had no intention of carrying out but which gave him the chance he sought of getting right away from his hated Nazi employers.

There must have been such who got an unlooked-for chance like this. Feeling so certain that we were on the brink of war, Vernon took a short spell of leave and went off to fish at Dulverton, but as the weather was quite unusually brilliant, and the fishing no good, he rested and this he enjoyed enormously. It was very hot that August; flowers and trees were growing luxuriantly, and even in our little London garden the flowers were brilliant. I joined Vernon for a quiet few days and, to my surprise, met a member of his staff who had arrived with his family to see us at our comfortable little hotel – he was also hoping to put in a few days enjoying the country, before getting down to the stresses and strain he knew must lie before him. He and Vernon had no illusions as to what an enormous pressure of work they would have to face, and though Vernon was always an optimist he knew, for he was also a realist, that the road that would lead to eventual victory would be hard and relentless. He never doubted that eventually, after a long struggle, we should win through.

Vernon had made many friends in Devonshire and Somerset and we often met them at the Staghound meets; it was such a friendly community. My sister arrived at Dulverton unexpectedly, and made our little party all the merrier for we carried on regardless of war talk. Our younger son and his wife went off in their car to France for a holiday. Vernon warned them not to, but they just laughed and thought it would be easy enough to get back, even if the war were to break out. Vernon thought not, but then wishful thinking mostly gets the better of good advice and off they went.

The holiday season was in full swing when we heard that Hitler had given orders for troops to march into Danzig and Poland – that decided it. Our government sent an ultimatum to Germany, and war was now inevitable. After the declaration of war on September 3rd everyone began to realise how unprepared we were to tackle so desperate a situation. The Germans were ready with their huge armies splendidly equipped, their air force heavily outnumbering ours, and their navy in full fighting trim. Our armies and our air force were quite inadequate both in size and equipment to meet the dangers that lay ahead. Only our navy was well prepared, we trusted much to that.

Vernon knew it would only be a matter of days now before we must expect an immense influx of refugees to arrive at the ports. They would have to be sifted, for among them would be many landing with the intention of making use of our hospitality to gather all the information they could for enemy use.[7] Should Hitler's submarine campaign succeed in gaining its objective, we should go very short of food and there would be so many extra people to feed. Rationing food was started from the first, that was all to the good; the scheme was well conceived and worked fairly for all alike. There was talk of invasion – that would be a horror we had not suffered since the Norman Conquest. It did not bear thinking about, but preparations had to be made, and the navy was ready.

When the first refugees began to pour in Vernon awaited their arrival with his plans to counter the dangers that he foresaw. In the First War these refugees were carefully examined at the ports of entry and all questionable people were sent to concentration camps, but in this war it was different. The crowds of fleeing people were allowed into our country so speedily that it was impossible to carry out these precautions, and therefore something different had to be devised. It was only after some little time had elapsed that very strict examinations could be carried out, and then combing was done very thoroughly.

Our Expeditionary Force was now leaving for France and with it the Territorial Regiment to which our younger son belonged. Vernon managed to come and see him off and drove down to join his wife who was returning with us to London. It was all rather a nightmare, for we knew how little training he had been having, which was also true of many of the others in his regiment. We wondered what would happen should they be called upon to do battle against splendidly equipped and highly trained troops. Vernon felt it was one of those gambles we have so often pulled off successfully, but would it come off this time? We all gaily said goodbye and then drove back to London with my daughter-in-law who had no illusions as to what her husband was facing – she knew it was pretty grim. I was glad Vernon had to work hard, and that I too, had plenty to do. The canteen in which I worked was for those in Vernon's office and for another government department as well. It was managed by Mrs Yapp, whose husband ran the Metropolitan Police canteen. She was quite indefatigable, and the many hundreds of people who had their meals in that canteen were well looked after. She was charming to work with.

At this time of such great anxiety Vernon often had long talks with Sir Robert Vansittart, later Lord Vansittart.[8] He envisaged so clearly the way the German mind works; he knew them well, and his advice was always pretty drastic. It was now October, and everything was still rather chaotic for as yet the war was in what came to be called the 'phoney' stage, and we had not been attacked. Then came the sinking of the *Royal Oak* with heavy loss of men, and this stirred us up to make greater efforts to meet the exigencies of what we now knew would have to be a very long war.

Letters from our son in France told us but little; we could only gather that all were watching and waiting for Hitler's next move. We expected air raids, but fortunately they did not materialise for some time, so giving us the chance to improve our plans for defence. Then came the news of the sinking of the HMS *Rawalpindi* and the gallant fight she put up against the

German pocket battleship *Deutschland*. It was a tale of war at sea which will go down in history as one of the bravest fights on record. They called them merchant cruisers, these lightly armed passenger ships that fought with all they had of speed and clever seamanship, to counter the efforts of the enemy to sink them. They gave a good account of themselves, and the *Rawalpindi* fame and that of her fearless captain helped us to set our teeth and bear stoically whatever lay in front of us.

In spite of things looking pretty black we still managed to lead a fairly ordinary life. We much enjoyed a lunch party arranged by Gilbert Wakefield. He and his wife Isabel Jeans[9] got a party together at the Garrick Club and asked such guests as Pilcher, Maud, Birkett, Monckton and Ivor Novello[10]. How well known many of those names have become now. It is tragic to think that Ivor Novello was to die so suddenly not many years after that. The Garrick Club is really historic and had a dignity and beauty all its own – some most interesting paintings of great actors fascinated us. Ivor Novello was the life and soul of the party and I could well understand that actors and actresses loved him. His generosity was proverbial and his kindness to young artists helped to encourage them in their careers. We came back from that party feeling much refreshed for we had been in touch, for a little while, with such a different world of artist thought, of gay adventure almost, and Vernon returned to his work quite light-heartedly.

He was dealing with a case at this time concerning a woman enemy agent.[11] She was discovered collecting information about certain south coast defences – she gave pretty accurate details of these and of the number of searchlights and anti-aircraft guns, and sent sketches relating to these defences. She was wearing a small swastika flag under the lapel of her coat – it would have been most useful had the Germans been successful in landing on our coast. She could then have posed as quite a heroine. But as things were, she had a criminal record and her spy activities had all been discovered; she had cut many telephone wires and had been responsible for several acts which could be described as fifth columnist. She was arrested and given a heavy sentence.

It was now nearly Christmastime, the weather was extremely cold, and there was dense fog for several days on end – no need to do any blacking out, as we were completely so already. Driving to and from the office was a nightmare. The closely packed traffic moved at a snail's pace, it was almost like being in a tunnel for you could barely see your hand in front of you. We managed to have a Christmas dinner at the office canteen, and another branch of our large community gave a big Christmas tree party and presents were handed out most generously to all and sundry. It was a real break in our busy days to have this gay afternoon – there was a splendid spirit everywhere, a spirit of camaraderie, which drew together the whole people. Good humour was infectious, never any grousing, for when the country is in danger we all pull together in a wonderful way. In Vernon's office this spirit was specially marked and as usual, if it was necessary to work all night without a break, it was done. There was something about Vernon himself that inspired that will to do and to help in every way possible. Even now, after many years have passed, I still hear it spoken of by those who knew and worked with him. He had a wonderful touch, partly I think because of his unfailing sympathy and understanding of all who served under him and with all those he came in contact with.

This was our first Christmas under war conditions, though the war could hardly be said to have done anything more than just scratch the surface of our living conditions. There was tenseness in the air, an expectation that was evident in everyone. We entered the year 1940 with high hopes, but with great anxieties too, for we knew how unprepared we were should the war be launched against our shores. An invasion! Well that was almost unthinkable. We listened to the rumours of German troops ready to march into Holland at any moment, and we knew that the French were still waiting and watching, trusting in their Maginot Line, which was acting like a drug and bogging down the efforts that should have been made to meet the eventual onrush of the enemy.

Influenza was taking its toll pretty heavily in northern France amongst the troops, and our son fell a victim, and pretty badly too. When he came home on sick leave he told us of the kindness and hospitality he had received in a French family, where the housekeeper nursed him devotedly night and day, with the help of his batman. When he sent our thanks to her and to the head of the house, with money to pay for all the many things they must have got for him, we received a letter saying that at one time there was great anxiety but Madame had applied her 'knowledge of nursing' and he had recovered well. She was enchanted with the food we were able to send them later on, some of which they could only get at exorbitant prices in France. The 'thank-you letter' from them was so warm-hearted that we were glad that we were able to make some little return for all their kindness to John.

Meanwhile our elder son had returned to the army feeling that, as a trained soldier, his place was there, and he could no longer stay at home in the War Department Constabulary. It was some months before he went abroad, and then we were not to see him for a very long time. After several moves he finally got to India, and was in the Imphal Campaign in what was called the Forgotten Army, namely the 14th Army, on the Assam Burma Border. He did not come home for over five years, during which time he had many adventures. Previous to his service in India he had to fight in Italian Somaliland with a small force he raised which gave a very good account of itself. Fortunately he could speak Arabic pretty fluently and had to do much translating for the officers in command of his troops who knew but little Arabic. When there was no further need for these very brave men, fighting in Somaliland having ceased, he went on to Syria, and from there to India where he served for a time under General Scoones[12] and later under General Slim.[13] He managed to send us letters from time to time but he could tell us little, and we could only guess at what he was doing.

He wrote home very thrilled when he heard of the birth of his little daughter, but it was to be a very long time before he could see her.[14]

27

RESIGNATION FROM MI5

❦

H ere, at home, things were beginning to look pretty grim.
I remember dining with Vernon in a beautiful house in Cheyne
Walk, where there were some very valuable pictures. Our
host remarked that he was expecting to have to sell them to the invading
Germans when they marched through London, and would need to barter
them for food for his friends in need. We thought this a bit pessimistic, but
our host was quite sure that we should shortly find the Germans landing
on the east coast and marching on to London in triumph! Yet another
friend felt equally certain that many of us would be put up against a wall
and shot. I laughed and said that in that case Vernon's chances of being
let off were slight, for his photograph had quite recently appeared in a
German newspaper with an account of what was known of his work. Yes,
he very evidently thought that disaster stared Vernon in the face in the
not-too-distant future.

A good many people had these same gloomy forebodings as to
invasion, and there was real clamour in the House of Commons. Neville
Chamberlain resigned on May 8th, and Winston Churchill became prime
minister the next day. The Germans were now invading Belgium and
Holland, and had started a war movement, for they had gone forwards
in amazingly quick marches, and in such numbers that we were left with

no choice but to evacuate the troops we had just sent over to Belgium. The weather was wonderful, the sea as calm as a millpond, and as our evacuation had not been anticipated our troops had to get back as best they could. The epic of that evacuation has been well told; how every available craft of every description large and small, even rowing boats, brought the men back from Dunkirk. It was almost a miracle that even the smallest boats could do this ferry work, and have no mishaps. But in France, on the way to Dunkirk, many of the troops had very tough fighting. My niece's husband Colonel Geoffrey Allen was killed; he was commanding a battalion of the Royal Fusiliers and was in the division holding back the enemy to allow the retreating troops to reach Dunkirk. She could hear no news, though she knew there had been heavy fighting. It was many weeks before she was told officially that he had been fatally wounded. How many there were in the same desperate plight as she, and how bravely these women faced the future, working day and night to help in whatever way they could, in the various services that had been started. She herself gladly undertook fire watching in London, and was always at her post. Some nights were a nightmare, but she worked well, thankful to be able to do her bit.

There was feverish activity in all government offices and Vernon found it easy to recruit most willing and expert help in keeping track of all questionable people who could make trouble. Spy stories of all kinds were pouring in: some absolutely ridiculous, some serious. One particularly stupid one was solemnly reported by a lady who said that she felt sure a neighbour of hers must be giving signals to the enemy, for she would hang out her washing in a pattern fitting a morse code: long short, short long, long long short, etc. Vernon could have kept a book of some of the absurd suggestions that came in hundreds of letters; there was a sort of spy mania as there had also been in the First World War. Everyone was in a tremendous state of anticipation as the Germans approached nearer and nearer to Calais. What would happen next? Were we indeed being sufficiently safeguarded against the activities of spies? This was the question in many official minds, for the country was in very grave danger. They felt that Vernon was growing old and had been a long time in the saddle, and a younger man might have some new ideas with which to tackle the dangerous work of those worming their way into the country. Perhaps they did not consider that it takes a very long time to become master in the art of counter-espionage. When Vernon realised what was in their minds he at once resigned and so, after many years of hard work undertaken with immense enthusiasm, he left with a heavy heart, for he knew that he could give much skilled service to his country in this time of great need. He hoped that a younger man would be able to do all the work with the vigour and insight that was needed to satisfy the demands that would be made upon him. I think the heroic qualities of Vernon's character came out more strongly than ever before in the manner with which he faced having to leave the work he really lived for. Of course he could not rest; he felt he must look around and see if there was something useful he could do in some new capacity. He heard of Lord Bessborough's[1] work for the Free French Welfare and joined that.[2] It was interesting and kept him busy.

There were days when the war news called for every bit of our British coolness, and the camaraderie which always unites us in times of danger kept us cheerful and ready to meet any emergencies. All of us, from the highest to the lowest, worked together with a will that no disasters could disturb. Even after the most devastating air raids, and ever-greater destruction and loss of life, this cheerfulness and helpfulness persisted. It was a matter of pride and fortitude to be in the office, or wherever one worked, on time, even when it seemed almost impossible. Although it was a strain on nerves and body this spirit of pride and resourcefulness made everyone consider it almost a privilege to be just one of the ordinary folk, doing just ordinary jobs with courage undaunted by the most alarming circumstances. There was plenty to laugh at too, if you could see the funny side of the many odd situations we met everywhere. I had advised our housekeeper, and another devoted woman who was helping us in our house, to sleep in the semi-basement, it being a little safer than upstairs. Our housekeeper was an exceptionally good sleeper, and she would dream happily through the most terrific raids, oblivious of whistling bombs, crashes and bangs of all sorts. Only once, when an extra-large bomb crashed quite close to the house and almost threw her out of bed, did she look at all alarmed and ask, 'What was that?' Well, what was it indeed? We laughed in utter surprise that she had heard nothing of the awful din going on all around us, for the night was hideous with noise. Our planes, though in such inferior numbers, were constantly attacking the enemy planes and our guns were barking out their defiance very inadequately in those early days, but quite indefatigably.

It was August and the Battle of Britain was being fought out. We felt so sure we should win through in the end though the odds were so much against us. It seemed incredible when Vernon brought me the news later on in September that our few planes were bringing down enemy planes in great numbers: one day 144 were mentioned, another as many as 150! He told me calmly that even these numbers were being exceeded and I could not believe it – and thought it was just wishful thinking! Probably the numbers were exaggerated, but it remained true that the German losses were enormous. Vernon would come to meet me when I was working at St James's Palace for the Red Cross, after he had been helping with the Free French Welfare work at one of our big London hotels – Lord Bessborough had been given office room there. He would tell me of our victories in the air and regard my incredulity with amusement for he knew what the truth was, namely that our few daring young pilots, with untiring intrepidity, had taken up their Spitfire planes time after time, all day and all night, and had indeed won the Battle of Britain which will go down in history as one of our finest.

Towards the end of September Vernon decided that, as our house had been made almost impossible to run, we should go into the country and he would try and get some more responsible work there. We therefore left for Buckingham where we stayed with the daughter of Colonel Warren, then Chief Constable of the county, and an old friend.[3] His daughter had lost her airman husband in one of our raids over Germany's north coast, and she was working in her father's office. She was glad to have someone to run her house and we could bring our housekeeper and maid to help in doing so. This turned out quite a good arrangement.

Vernon joined the local special constabulary and helped in Olney police station. Not much to do, but something to be interested in while he tried to find a suitable job further afield. In the evenings we would listen eagerly to the news, for those were the days when Winston Churchill's speeches on the radio were the tonic that kept us going. After listening to him we felt, as all did, braced for every and any emergency. He would put quite a different complexion on everything and was a stimulus greater than anything else could have been.

We could take heart again to make the best of even inactivity, which was Vernon's special cross to bear. As usual he gained friends very quickly; the police in particular, in the local office where he worked, would do anything for him. He tried to join in whatever organisation the local people were preparing, to meet any dangers that might come to our locality. He would attend certain conferences and give lectures occasionally on whatever portion of his previous work could be safely given.

On his visits to London he would be told of some startling cases. One of these really distressed him for it concerned an Englishman.[4] It was rare to find one willing to spy for his country's enemies, but this man had lost all sense of decency and had a bad criminal record. He had originally worked as a low-grade engineer in cargo ships plying on Atlantic and Far Eastern routes. He had served several prison sentences – one in the United States Penitentiary – mostly for false pretences, larceny, house breaking, and so on. He managed to obtain work without troubling to get the necessary labour permit, and was eventually deported from the USA. But before this occurred he thought out a plan of making what he considered was 'easy money'; namely, to offer his services to the German consul to act as a spy in England. He managed to get his letter smuggled out of Massachusetts where he then lived. Unfortunately for him it was discovered and the addressee never received it; instead it was given to a British government official who sent it to England. When this man reached Cardiff after being deported he had every intention of starting his easy-money career, and was amazed when he was arrested. In the annals of history this man will go down as the first British subject to be convicted under the Treachery Act of 1940.[5] Vernon listened to many other tales, both brave and knavish, of spies and would-be spies, but this one of an Englishman was much the most despicable.

After his many tours and lectures at various places, Vernon would return to tell us of what he had heard of victories in Libya and of the hope that it might be possible for us to send out a really fine striking force to France in the not-too-distant future. He gave me a graphic description of the destruction caused by the air raids in London: the ruin of the Temple Church and the effect of the incendiary bombs in the St Paul's Cathedral area. Londoners seemed quite inured to bomb attacks and there was the strongest feeling of optimism, for things were certainly improving and we were sure that victory was coming. We ourselves could hear the enemy bombers come over most nights in the midlands, and we could see the flares from our windows during the attacks. The night of the Coventry raid was the worst; the droning of the enemy bombers went on for hours, they seemed to come over in hundreds, and fires lit up the sky for miles around. It was a ghastly night but we only realised next day how very terrible it had been. Those of us living away from London were not so completely filled with that spirit of confidence which was so marked among the people in London itself, especially after such devastation as had just taken place at Coventry. But a stirring speech by Winston Churchill could make that spirit glow, and throughout the country, confidence and strength would be stimulated with even greater vigour.

That winter of 1941 was bitter cold and roads were often flooded with melting snow. Vernon and our hostess had bought a little second-hand car between them so that we should not feel too marooned, though the snow defeated us on many occasions. Vernon was now elected chairman of the Local Emergency Committee, for it was necessary to have some plans ready to counter the effects of such bombing as had taken place only a few miles away from us. In September he went off to Hampshire to see our younger son who was training at Larkhill, where he found everyone imbued with the Montgomery spirit of keen preparation for the day when all was to be in perfect readiness for the attack on France.[6] He described how electrifying those visits of General Montgomery were, when he would come for inspection, and the enthusiasm he created, and the cheerfulness with which the rigorous training he demanded was carried out. In winter the men slept out in frost and snow, done with a keen sense of the necessity of making them tough, also learning to be fully competent to carry out on each man's own responsibility, whatever task was required of him. What a difference from his experience of the first few months of the war when he went out to France quite untrained and unfit. Vernon was intensely interested in the new training ideas that were being carried out, and which had not as yet been fully developed. He knew we were not going to move till we were absolutely ready, and his admiration for the methods of General Montgomery was unbounded. After visiting many old haunts and meeting his friends he would arrive home in our tiny village much cheered by all he had seen and by the spirit of confidence everywhere. At a Sunday parade of special constables in Buckingham he was asked to address the men on one of his special subjects, that of quick observation. He certainly had the gift of saying what captured the attention of those listening to him, and could work up much enthusiasm for whatever he wished them to appreciate. He enjoyed lecturing and was in much request.

His work at Olney police station amused him, and he would laugh and say he hoped he was satisfactory. He would go off first thing in the morning in the little car, which was most temperamental and had a remarkable talent for jibbing like a bucking horse, especially on cold mornings. Then no amount of coaxing or pushing would induce the engine to start until suddenly, for no apparent reason, the car would plunge forward and go off with no further bother. Then all assistants would wave goodbye amidst much laughter, and Vernon would be off to the police station. We had a great affection for this little second-hand car; it took us about everywhere, petrol permitting, for we were very tightly rationed.

In the spring of 1942 it was still very cold; we had had three years of quite unusually cold winters with constant snow and ice. We could keep very warm in the little house we lived in, but outside it was piercingly cold, the more so as we were near the River Ouse. In good weather it was good fun to be so near, for we could carry down our fishing tackle and Vernon, like all good fisherman, always hoped to be successful, though that sluggish river gave very little chance of much sport. But in winter our close proximity to the river made the cold more penetrating, and we would come back in the evening to sit gratefully by a blazing fire and wait for the six o'clock news. Then Vernon would eagerly listen, hoping to hear something that would bring the longed-for victory a little nearer, and I would realise what his unwilling inactivity meant to him.

One day he went off as usual to the police station but returned early – he complained of a bad pain in his chest. He had caught a cold, which turned to pleurisy and pneumonia, and he did not recover.

He had so eagerly looked forward to the time when at last the conquered and conquerors would meet together on either side of a table, to work out something between them that might lead to a lasting peace. This was the question: would it, or could it, ever be a lasting peace? Vernon feared that the world must grow very much older in experience and wisdom before this could be achieved. He did not know of the atomic weapons and the hydrogen bomb which were later developed – weapons so terrible that the fear of their use may prove to be the power that will prevent war on a big scale. But he was sure that fear must not be our only deterrent, and that something much higher and better than that must come to work the miracle of PEACE.

NOTES

❖

1 Moscow

1   The Committee of Imperial Defence (CID) was an ad hoc part of the British government from 1902 to 1939, responsible for research on matters of defence policy. Typically, a temporary sub-committee would be established to investigate and report on a particular issue, such as the Sub-Committee on Foreign Espionage in 1909, which recommended the establishment of the Secret Service Bureau (SSB).

2   A Yarmouth bloater is a type of whole cold-smoked herring, salted and lightly smoked without gutting. They are distinct from kippers: kippers are split smoked herring, bloaters are cured whole herring that have not been split open.

3   Georgina Kell (née Konarska) (1855–no date available). Born in Brussels, Belgium.

4   Dr Samuel Konarski (born Praszka, Poland 1803–died Nice, France 1893). A doctor by profession, he fought in the Polish–Russian War of 1830 as an officer of the 1ˢᵗ Podhalian Rifle Regiment.

5   Robert Gascoyne-Cecil (1830–1903), 3ʳᵈ Marquess of Salisbury. Conservative Prime Minister 1885–1886, 1886–1892 and 1895–1902.

6   Colonel William Kenyon-Slaney (1847–1908), army officer and Conservative MP for the Newport division of Shropshire 1886–1908. Kenyon-Slaney was an outstanding sportsman who played football for England and cricket for the Marylebone Cricket Club.

7   Major Waldegrave CF Kell (1850–1915). Divorced from Vernon Kell's mother in 1892.

8   The Connaught Rangers were an Irish line infantry regiment of the British Army from 1881 to 1922, formed when the 88ᵗʰ Foot (Connaught Rangers) and 94ᵗʰ Foot were amalgamated.

9   The Anglo-Zulu War of January 1879–July 1879 was fought between the British Empire and the Zulu Kingdom. British victory ended the Zulu nation's independence.

10   Napoléon Eugène Louis Jean Joseph Bonaparte (1856–1879), eldest son of French Emperor Napoleon III, and known as Prince Imperial. He settled in England after his father was dethroned in 1870, served as a Lieutenant in the British Army, and was ambushed and killed while part of a forward scouting party.

11   Eugénie de Montijo (1826–1920), Empress Consort of France 1853–1871.

12   The South Staffordshire Regiment was a line infantry regiment of the British Army from 1881 to 1959, when it was amalgamated with the North Staffordshire Regiment to form the Staffordshire Regiment. The headquarters were at Whittington Barracks, Lichfield. Since 2007 the Staffordshire Regiment has been part of the Mercian Regiment.

13   The Royal Military Academy (RMA), Sandhurst, Berkshire is where the British Army trains its officers. Until 1939 infantry and cavalry officers were trained at Sandhurst; artillery, engineers, signals and other technical corps undertook officer training at RMA, Woolwich.

14   Sir Winston Churchill (1874–1965), Liberal Home Secretary February 1910–October 1911, and Conservative Prime Minister 1940–1945 and 1951–1955.

15   Lilla Girard Kell (née Mitchell) (1858–1911) married Waldegrave Kell in 1894. In 1913, Waldegrave Kell married Kathleen Sophie Kell (née Lett) (date of birth not known–1946).

16   Agent for the White Star Line, which owned the RMS *Titanic*.

2 Journey Through Canada

1   The Jameson Raid took place over the New Year weekend of 29 December 1895–2 January 1896. It was a botched raid on the Transvaal Republic commanded by Sir Leander Jameson, the 2nd Administrator of Rhodesia 1894–1896. His troops were police employed by Cecil Rhodes' British South Africa Company and Bechuanaland police. Jameson aimed to incite an uprising among the primarily British expatriate workers (Uitlanders) in Transvaal. The Raid failed and there was no

uprising. However, the Jameson Raid was an inciting factor in the Second Boer War.

2   In the Second Boer War (or South African War) 1899–1902, the UK fought against the South African Republic (Transvaal Republic) and the Orange Free State. The First Boer war was fought in 1880–1881.

3   Major-General Sir John Ardagh (1840–1907), Director of Military Intelligence 1896–1901.

4   Theodore Roosevelt (1858–1919), Governor of New York State January 1899–December 1900 and Republican President of the United States 1901–1909.

4 Shanghai and Active Service

1   Founded in the 1890s, the Big Sword Society was a traditional peasant self-defence group widespread in Northern China during the Qing Dynasty, consisting of local groups of smallholders and tenant farmers organised to defend their villages against roaming bandits and warlords. Noted for their reckless courage, the Grand Masters claimed to make their members invulnerable to bullets by magic.

2   Westerners referred to these well-trained and athletic young men as 'The Boxers' because of the martial arts and calisthenics they practised.

3   Major-General Sir Hamilton Bower (1858–1940). Bower wrote about his travels through Chinese Turkestan and Tibet. He raised and commanded the 1st Chinese Regiment at Wei-Hei-Wei in 1898 and fought in the relief of Tientsin and the relief of Peking.

4   Major-General Sir Arthur Dorward (1848–1934).

5   The Seymour Expedition was an attempt by a multinational military force to march to Peking and protect the diplomatic legations and foreign nationals there from attacks by Boxers in 1900. The Chinese Army defeated Seymour's expedition and forced it to return to Tientsin.

6   An Aide-de-Camp (ADC) is an assistant to a senior military or government official.

7   Sir Sidney Barton (1876–1946) was a British career diplomat. From 1899 to 1901 he was posted on special service to the British territory of

Wei-Hei-Wei and served as an interpreter and assistant political officer during the Boxer Rebellion. Appointed Consul-General to Shanghai in 1922 and later Minister to Abyssinia in 1929.

8   Admiral George Holmes Borrett (1868–1952).

5 Boxer Rebellion

1   A legation is a diplomatic representative office lower than an embassy, and headed by a minister. The Legation Quarter was an area in Peking where a number of foreign legations were located from 1861 to 1959, immediately to the East of Tiananmen Square. The Legation Quarter was encircled by a wall, which made it effectively a city within the city exclusively for foreigners. Many Chinese nationalists resented the Legation Quarter as a symbol of foreign dominance over China.

2   Empress Dowager Cixi (1835–1908), Empress Dowager and Regent who effectively controlled the Chinese Government from 1861 to 1909.

3   Admiral of the Fleet Sir Edward Hobart Seymour (1840–1929), Commander-in-Chief of the China Station 1897–1901.

4   General Sir Alfred Gaselee (1844–1918) of the Indian Army was chosen to command the British element of the international expeditionary force to China in the summer of 1900, known as the Gaselee Expedition, which succeeded in reaching Peking and relieving the diplomatic legations.

6 Relief of Peking

1   Bishop Charles Perry Scott (1847–1927), Anglican Bishop in North China 1880–1913. Married Frances Emily Burrows in 1889, daughter of Oxford University historian Montagu Burrows.

2   Captain Robert Falcon Scott (1868–1912), naval officer and Antarctic explorer. HMS *Terrible* was a protected cruiser, which served on the China Station from 1895 to 1904 and took part in suppressing the Boxer Rebellion.

3   Admiral Sir Ernest Gaunt (1965–1940) served as commissioner and superintending transport officer at Wei-Hei-Wei at the time of the Boxer Rebellion.

4   Admiral of the Fleet John Jellicoe (1859–1935), 1ˢᵗ Earl Jellicoe. Served as chief of staff to Admiral Seymour during the Seymour Expedition. Commanded the Grand Fleet from August 1914 to November 1916, including the Battle of Jutland in May 1916, and First Sea Lord from November 1916 to January 1918.

5   Colonel Sir Claude MacDonald (1852–1915), retired from the army in 1896 and was appointed British Minister in Peking. As a military man MacDonald led the defence of the foreign legations. In 1900 he was appointed Consul-General to Japan.

6   Lieutenant-General Sir Thomas Edwin Scott (1867–1937), British representative ('Resident') at the Aden Settlement 1921–1925.

7   The Eight-Nation Alliance was an international coalition set up in response to the Boxer Rebellion by Japan, Russia, the British Empire, France, USA, Germany, Italy, and Austria-Hungary. They launched what they perceived as a humanitarian intervention and invaded China, relieving the siege of the legations in Peking during summer 1900.

8   Field Marshal Alfred von Waldersee (1832–1905), Chief Imperial German General Staff 1888–1891 and Allied Supreme Commander in China 1900–1901.

7 Tientsin

1   Pierre-Marie-Alphonse Favier (1837–1905), French, Roman Catholic Lazarite Vicar Apostolic of Northern Hi-Li, China and titular bishop of Pentacomia 1899–1905. During the Boxer Rebellion, Favier was responsible for the preservation of Xishiku Cathedral, commonly referred to as the Beitang (the North Cathedral) in Peking.

2   Clemens von Ketteler (1853–1900), German plenipotentiary at Peking 1899–1900.

3   Lieutenant-General Sir James Grierson (1859–1914), Director of Military Operations (which included intelligence at that time) 1904–1906.

4   German Emperor Kaiser Wilhelm II (1859–1941), reigned 1888–1918, eldest grandchild of Britain's Queen Victoria.

5   Field Marshal Frederick Sleigh Roberts (1832–1914), 1st Earl Roberts. Awarded the Victoria Cross for gallantry in the Indian Mutiny of 1857. Commanded British troops during the 2nd Anglo-Boer War. Last Commander-in-Chief of the Forces, 1901–1904, after which the post was abolished and the post of Chief of the General Staff was created.

6   General Maharajah Sir Ganga Singh of Bikaner (1880–1943), commanded the Bikaner Camel Corps in the 1901 Chinese Campaign. Member of the British Imperial War Cabinet during the First World War, representing British-held India.

7   Field Marshal William Riddell Birdwood, 1st Baron Birdwood (1865–1951), Commander-in-Chief India 1925–1930. A distinguished commander of ANZAC (Australian and New Zealand) troops at Gallipoli and on the Western Front during the First World War. Married to Janetta Birdwood (née Bromhead), daughter of Colonel Sir Benjamin Bromhead of the Indian Army.

8   Maharajah Lieutenant-General Sir Pertab Singh of Idar (1845–1922), commanded the Jodhpur contingent during the Boxer Rebellion.

9   Maharajah Sir Madho Rao Scindia of Gwalior (1876–1925), appointed as an honorary ADC to King Edward VI in 1901 in recognition of his support during the Boxer Rebellion.

8 Visit to Tangshan

1   Major-General Lionel Dunsterville (1865–1946), led the so-called Dunsterforce across present-day Iran and Iraq towards the Caucasus and oil-rich Baku from December 1917 to September 1918. He went to school with Rudyard Kipling at the United Services College.

2   *Stalky & Co* is a novel by Rudyard Kipling, first published in 1899, about adolescent boys at a British boarding school. Stalky knows that he is destined for Sandhurst, so he does not care much about many academic subjects, and later proves to be brilliant in battle.

3   Herbert Hoover (1874–1964), Republican US President 1929–1933. A Quaker and mining engineer, Hoover led the US Food Administration during the First World War and became internationally recognised for his humanitarian relief efforts in war-torn Belgium. He was the first

US President to donate all his salary to charity. Despite his efforts, the US economy plummeted after the Wall Street Crash of 1929. At the time of the Boxer Rebellion, Hoover was the Chief Engineer for the Chinese Bureau of Mines. He and his wife both learned Mandarin Chinese during their time in China, and when he became President they spoke in Chinese in order to foil eavesdroppers in the White House.

11 A Distinguished Visitor

1   Taoism (also called Daoism) is a spiritual, philosophical and religious tradition of Chinese origin that emphasises living in harmony with the Tao. Tao means 'way', 'path', or 'principle'; Taoism means 'teaching of the way'. In Taoism, Tao denotes something that is both the source of, and the force behind, everything that exists.

2   Philosophical Taoism was founded by the ancient Chinese philosopher Lao-Tzu (usually dated around 6th century BC), a legendary figure and author of the *Tao Te Ching*.

3   The Society for the Propagation of the Gospel in Foreign Parts, founded in 1701, is an overseas missionary organisation of the Church of England, which expanded to China in 1863. It was more clearly focused on the promotion and support of indigenous Anglican churches and the training of local church leadership than the supervision and care of colonial and expatriate church congregations.

4   General Jean-Baptiste Marchand (1863–1934), French military officer and explorer in Africa. Marchand fought with the French expeditionary force in China during the Boxer Rebellion. He was best known for commanding the French expeditionary force during the Fashoda Incident of 1898, the climax of imperial territorial disputes between Britain and France in East Africa.

5   Li Hung-Chang (1823–1901) was a politician, general and diplomat of the late Qing dynasty. Best known in the West for his pro-modern stance and as a negotiator, he antagonised Britain with his support for Russia as a foil against Japanese expansion in Manchuria. He fell from favour with the Chinese after the loss of the Sino-Japanese War in 1894.

12 Shan-Hai-Kuan Reverts to Chinese Control

1   Viceroys governed one or more provinces of China during the Qing
    dynasty. The Viceroy of Mukden governed the three north-eastern
    provinces of Fengtian, Jilin and Heilongjiang.
2   Emperor Guangxu (1871–1908), reigned 1875–1908. In practice he only
    ruled, under Empress Dowager Cixi's influence, from 1889–1898. He
    initiated the Hundred Days' Reform, but was abruptly stopped when Cixi
    launched a coup in 1898 and kept him under house arrest until his death.
    Emperor Guangxu was killed by arsenic poisoning. There is speculation that
    Cixi knew that her own death was imminent and poisoned him so that she
    would be succeeded by her choice of heir and Emperor Guangxu would not
    continue his reforms. Cixi gave him food laced with arsenic and he dutifully
    ate it knowing that it would kill him. She died the day after him.

14 Farewell

1   James Vernon Waldegrave Kell (1901–1968), eldest son of Sir Vernon
    and Lady Kell.

16 Home Again

1   Walter Moresby was a barrister and joined MI5 as legal adviser on 9
    October 1914.
2   Margaret Vera Kell (1905–1940), daughter of Sir Vernon and Lady Kell.
3   Lieutenant-General Sir Francis Davies (1864–1948), Deputy Assistant
    Quartermaster General 1902–1904 and Assistant Director of Military
    Operations 1904–1907.
4   Brigadier-General Sir James Edmonds (1861–1956), head of MO5
    (Military Operations Directorate 5) from 1907 to 1910, and later Director
    of the Historical Section of the CID, responsible for the compilation of the
    28-volume official *History of the Great War*, eventually completed in 1949.
    Edmonds wrote 11 of the 14 volumes covering the Western Front himself.
5   Herbert Asquith (1852–1928), 1st Earl of Oxford and Asquith, Liberal
    Prime Minister 1908–1916.

6   Reginald Brabazon (1841–1929), 12th Earl of Meath, philanthropist and prominent Conservative politician in the House of Lords.

7   Field Marshal John French (1852–1925), 1st Earl of Ypres, Commander-in-Chief of the British Expeditionary Force (BEF) from August 1914 to December 1915.

8   Richard Burdon Haldane (1856–1928), 1st Viscount Haldane, Liberal Secretary of State for War 1905–1912 and Lord Chancellor 1912–1915. He was forced to resign as Lord Chancellor because of his perceived pro-German sympathies.

9   Sir Walter Hillier (1849–1927) was a British diplomat. He retired in 1896 as Consul-General in Seoul. From February to April 1901 he was called out of retirement and attached to the legation in Peking as special political officer for Chinese affairs. From 1904 to 1908, Hillier was a professor of Chinese at King's College University in London.

10   Edward Hillier (1857–1924), who lost his sight in 1896, was the Hong Kong and Shanghai Banking Corporation's (HSBC) agent in Peking.

11   Prince Luigi Amedeo (1873–1933), Duke of the Abruzzi, an Italian mountaineer and explorer known for his 1909 expedition to Mount K2.

12   Lieutenant-General Sir George Macdonogh (1865–1942), Director of Military Intelligence from 1916 to 1918 and Adjutant-General 1918–1922.

13   Admiral Frederick Dundas Gilpin-Brown (1866–1934).

14   John Gilpin is a literary character from William Cowper's 1782 comic ballad 'The Diverting History of John Gilpin'; a poem which tells how Gilpin became separated from his wife and children on a journey to the Bell Inn, Edmonton after Gilpin lost control of his horse and was carried 10 miles further to the town of Ware.

17 New Plans

1   Lieutenant Siegfried Helm was tried in September 1910. Helm pleaded guilty, but claimed that he had been sketching for his own amusement and not for the purposes of espionage, and was merely bound over and discharged. Under the Official Secrets Act (OSA) of 1889, it was necessary for the prosecution to prove intent to obtain information illegally.

2   Dr Max Schultz was sentenced to 21 months' imprisonment in
     November 1911. His espionage was detected when a local solicitor whom
     he tried to recruit as an agent reported him to the police.

3   Major Frederick Stanley Clarke (1875–1946) served in MI5 from January
     1911 to December 1912, before moving on to become Deputy Chief
     Constable of Kent Police. He was Chief Constable of Gloucestershire
     Police from 1918–1937.

4   Colonel Reginald Drake served as head of MI5's investigative branch
     from April 1912 to March 1917, before being appointed head of secret
     service work for the BEF.

5   K wrote in special brown ink. His successors do not refer to themselves as
     K or use this same ink. Cumming was known as C and wrote in special
     green ink. Even today the Chief of SIS is still known as C and writes in
     the same green ink that Cumming used.

6   Rear-Admiral John Moresby (1830–1922) married Jane Willis Scott
     of Queenstown, Ireland in 1859. Moresby made hydrological surveys
     around eastern New Guinea, discovering the harbour that he named
     Fairfax after his father. The town established there was called Port
     Moresby and is now the nation's capital.

7   Prince Henry of Prussia (1862–1929), a younger brother of Kaiser
     Wilhelm II, was a career naval officer who commanded Germany's Baltic
     Fleet during the First World War. He had a keen interest in motorcars
     and the Prince Heinrich Tour, a precursor of the German Grand Prix,
     was established in his honour in 1909.

8   The Royal Automobile Club (RAC), established in 1897, is a private
     British club for automobile enthusiasts.

9   MI5's Registry handled the collation, indexing and filing of all information
     received. In the words of an MI5 report from 1921, the Registry was 'the
     mainspring of the DEFENCE SECURITY INTELLIGENCE BUREAU
     and the basis of all useful Counter-Espionage work'.

10   Heinrich Grosse, alias Captain Hugh Grant, had served as a first
     officer in the German merchant navy. In November 1911, Portsmouth
     Dockyard Police informed MI5 that a man calling himself Captain Hugh
     Grant had attempted to solicit information about naval matters from a
     naval pensioner, William Salter, who reported him to the police. Grosse
     was sentenced to three years' penal servitude in February 1912.

11 Alberto Rosso (alias Albert Celso Rodriguez), was detected because he sent a telegram to a well-known spy address, and interned under the ARO on 3 August 1914.

12 In January 1913 George Parrott, chief gunner on HMS *Agamemnon*, was sentenced to four years' imprisonment for passing 23 classified Royal Navy manuals to the German secret service. His espionage was detected by the interception of intermediary Walter Kruger's correspondence in December 1911.

13 Sir Basil Thomson (1861–1939), son of the Archbishop of York and a trained barrister, had a varied career as a colonial administrator, writer and prison governor. From June 1913 to 1921, as the Metropolitan Police's Assistant Commissioner (Crime), Thomson was head of the CID, which included the Special Branch that worked very closely with MI5. From 1919 to 1921 he also held the position of Director of Intelligence at the Home Office, which put him in overall charge of every British intelligence agency.

14 Armgaard Karl Graves was sentenced to 18 months' imprisonment for espionage in July 1912. His spying was detected by intercepting the post to a known intermediary for the German secret service. Graves volunteered to become a British double agent. Kell agreed and Graves was released from prison in December 1912. Kell planned to send Graves on a mission to Berlin but, having been paid in advance by MI5, Graves absconded to the USA. Graves repeatedly wired to MI5 asking for more money until Kell cut him off. In 1914 Graves caused considerable embarrassment to MI5 by publishing sensational accounts of his career as a spy for the Germans and the British in American newspapers.

18 Some Fruition

1 Adolphe Pegoud (1899–1915), French aviator who became the first fighter ace during the First World War.

2 Hugh Fortescue Locke King (1848–1926), British entrepreneur who founded and financed Brooklands motor racing circuit in Weybridge, Surrey.

3 Louis Bleriot (1872–1936), French aviator, inventor and engineer.

4   Gustav Hamel (1889–1914), a pioneer aviator of British nationality who was born in Germany.

5   George Breckow, alias Reginald Rowland, was a naturalised US citizen of German birth, who had worked in the piano export business in America. His espionage was detected by a check on the known spy address Dierks & Co, and he was shot on 26 October 1915.

6   Louise Wertheim (née Klitschke), a German Pole by birth who became a British subject by marriage to Bruno Wertheim, was sentenced to 10 years' penal servitude.

7   Rather than communicating directly with their agents in the UK, the German secret service communicated via intermediaries ('post boxes') in the UK who passed these communications on to the agents.

8   The interception of Croner's letters revealed that Karl Gustav Ernst was an intermediary for the German secret service.

9   Arthur Neville Chamberlain (1869–1940), Conservative Prime Minister from May 1937 to May 1940. Best known for his appeasement policy, particularly signing the 1938 Munich Agreement, conceding the Sudetenland region of Czechoslovakia to Germany. In 1912, Chamberlain was a Liberal Unionist member of Birmingham City Council for All Saint's ward, located within his father's parliamentary constituency.

10   Brigadier-General Sir Eric Holt-Wilson (1875–1950), Deputy-Director of MI5 until 1940.

11   Lieutenant-General Sir Arthur Lyttelton-Annesley (1837–1926), Commander-in-Chief Scotland 1888–1893.

12   William Klare was sentenced to five years' imprisonment for espionage in June 1913. He was detected when one of his letters to Steinhauer was intercepted. Steinahuer had tasked Klare with obtaining a confidential report. Klare, a dentist, used the metaphor of transporting a patient to Ostend to refer to this report in his correspondence.

19 War

1   Archduke Franz Ferdinand of Austria (1863–1914), heir presumptive to the Austro-Hungarian throne. His assassination by Serb nationalists in Sarajevo on 28 June 1914 precipitated Austro-Hungary's declaration

of war on Serbia, which soon escalated into the First World War as the Central Powers and Serbia's allies declared war on each other.

2   Lieutenant-Colonel Maldwyn Haldane was head of MI5's Organisation, Administration and Records branch during the First World War.

3   Walter Rimann had been added to the Special War List for arrest upon the outbreak of war, but he got away by leaving for Zeebrugge on 1 August 1914.

4   Field Marshal Horatio Herbert Kitchener (1850–1916), 1st Earl Kitchener, was Secretary of State for War from August 1914 to June 1916.

5   Lieutenant Alastair Smith Cumming, of the Seaforth Highlanders and attached to the Intelligence Corps, died in a motor accident on 3 October 1924, aged 24.

6   Captain Sir Mansfield Smith Cumming (1859–1923), Chief of the Foreign Section of the Secret Service Bureau from 1909 to 1923, known as MI1c during the First World War and today known as the Secret Intelligence Service (SIS) or MI6. Cumming's leg was amputated the next day. He often shocked his subordinates during meetings by suddenly stabbing his artificial leg with a letter opener as a way of emphasising the point that he was making.

7   It is not clear which German agent is being referred to here. A number of German spies, such as Carl Lody, used lemon juice as a secret ink in the early days of the First World War, until it was superseded by secret inks that were harder to detect.

8   Gustav Steinhauer (1870–1930), head of the British section of the German Admiralty's intelligence service, the Nachrichten-Abteilung, from 1901 to 1914.

9   Reimers was one of the cover addresses that Steinhauer used to communicate with his agents in Britain.

10   Lieutenant Carl Lody (1877–1914), his espionage was detected by postal interception and he was shot in the Tower of London on 6 November 1914.

11   The RMS *Lusitania*, a British ocean liner, was sunk by a German submarine on 7 May 1915. In firing on a non-military vessel without warning, the Germans breached the international laws known as the Cruiser Rules. A total of 128 American citizens died, unleashing a storm of anti-German feeling in the USA.

12 Founded in 1909, the Voluntary Aid Detachment (VAD) was a voluntary unit providing field nursing services throughout the UK and other parts of the British Empire. Most volunteers came from the middle and upper classes. During the First World War, 38,000 VADs worked in hospitals and as ambulance drivers and cooks. Famous female VADs include Agatha Christie, Hattie Jacques, Amelia Earhart and Vera Brittain. Female VADs over 23 years of age and with more than three months' hospital experience were accepted for overseas service.

13 Miss EA Lomax was Lady Superintendent of the Registry during the First World War. She was awarded an MBE in 1918 and then an OBE in 1920.

20 Air Raids

1 Ben Tillett (1880–1943), British socialist, trade union leader and politician, was a Labour MP from 1917 to 1924 and 1929 to 1931. Tillett courted controversy with some Labour supporters through his outspoken support for Britain's involvement in the First World War, an issue that split the Labour Party.

2 Henry Manners (1852–1925), 8th Duke of Rutland, a Conservative MP from 1888 to 1895 until his elevation to the House of Lords, and Lord-Lieutenant of Leicestershire from 1900 to 1925.

3 Wing Commander Neville Usborne (1883–1916) of the Royal Naval Air Service (RNAS) played a prominent part in British lighter-than-air aviation before the First World War, being involved in the construction of His Majesty's Airship number 1, 'Mayfly', an aerial scout airship. He was killed during an early experiment launching an aeroplane from an airship in flight.

4 Admiral of the Fleet John ('Jackie') Fisher (1841–1920), 1st Baron Fisher, First Sea Lord 1904–1910 and 1914–1915.

5 Vice-Admiral Cecil Usborne (1880–1951), Director of Naval Intelligence (DNI) from 1930 to 1932.

6 Commander Sir Charles Dennistoun Burney (1888–1968), naval officer, Conservative MP, aeronautical engineer and inventor.

7   Haicke Janssen and Wilhelm Roos, both Dutch citizens, were German
    agents who came to the UK posing as cigar merchants. They were detected
    by telegrams to a known spy address and both shot on 30 July 1915.

8   Robert Rosenthal, who posed as an American travelling salesman selling
    gas lighters, was hanged on 16 July 1915. He was detected when the
    censorship discovered secret writing in one of his letters.

21 Return to London

1   Frederick William Sanderson (1857–1922), education reformer who
    introduced innovative programmes of education in engineering, and
    headmaster of Oundle School from 1892 to 1922.

2   Dr Thomas Arnold (1795–1842), headmaster of Rugby School from
    1828 to 1841 where he introduced a number of reforms.

3   Manfred von Richthofen (1892–1918), First World War German fighter
    ace, who commanded Jagdgeschwader I, better known as the 'Flying
    Circus'.

4   Émile Jaques-Dalcroze (1865–1950), Swiss composer, musician and music
    educator. He developed Dalcroze Eurhythmics – a method of learning
    and experiencing music through movement.

5   Brigadier-General Sir George Kynaston Cockerill (1867–1957), Deputy
    Director of Military Intelligence and Director of Special Intelligence (in
    charge of the Sub-Directorate of Special Intelligence comprising MI5,
    MI6, MI7, MI8 & MI9) during the First World War and a Conservative
    MP from 1918 to 1931.

6   Admiral Sir William Reginald 'Blinker' Hall (1870–1943), Director
    of Naval Intelligence (DNI) during the First World War, and a
    Conservative MP 1919–1923 and 1925–1929. The Naval Intelligence
    Division (NID) was arguably the pre-eminent British intelligence
    agency during the First World War. Hall was responsible, with Alfred
    Ewing, for establishing the Royal Navy's codebreaking unit, Room 40,
    which decoded the infamous Zimmermann Telegram, a major factor in
    the USA's entry into the war.

7   Admiral of the Fleet Sir Fairfax Moresby (1786–1877), Commander-in-
    Chief Pacific Station 1850–1853.

22 War Ending

1   Arthur Balfour (1848–1930), 1st Earl Balfour, Conservative Prime Minister 1902–1905, First Lord of the Admiralty May 1915–December 1916 and Foreign Secretary December 1916–October 1919.

2   Guglielmo Marconi (1874–1937), Italian electrical engineer, inventor and entrepreneur. He shared the 1909 Nobel Prize in Physics with Karl Braun in recognition of their contributions to the development of wireless telegraphy.

3   Big Bertha was a German howitzer used against the Liège forts in 1914. The long-range siege gun that the Germans used to shell Paris from March to August 1918 was actually nicknamed the Paris Gun;, however the French wrongly referred to it as Big Bertha.

4   Marshal Ferdinand Foch (1851–1929), French general and Allied supreme commander from March 1918 to November 1918.

5   Georges Clemenceau (1841–1929), French Prime Minister 1906–1909 and 1917–1920.

6   Woodrow Wilson (1856–1924), Democratic US President 1913–1921. Wilson was awarded the Nobel Peace Prize in 1919 for his sponsorship of the League of Nations. A devoted Presbyterian, Wilson infused morality into his internationalism – an activist foreign policy calling on the USA to promote global democracy.

7   Wilson's Fourteen Points took many of his progressive domestic ideas and translated them into a progressive foreign policy, which he saw as the only possible basis for an enduring peace: free trade, open diplomacy, democracy and self-determination.

8   The worldwide H1M1 flu pandemic from January 1918 to December 1920, known as the Spanish influenza, was one of the deadliest natural disasters in human history, infecting 500 million people and resulting in between 50 and 100 million deaths, 3–5 per cent of the world's population.

9   The post-war demobilisation of the British Army was handled very badly. The authorities did not adopt the sensible policy of first in first out, creating a sense of injustice, which led to mutinies at army camps in Folkestone and Calais in late-1918 and early-1919. MI5 reports linked some of these troubles with pro-Soviet agitators.

10   On 24 March 1919 MI5 celebrated victory in the Great War with the
     'Hush-Hush' revue and dinner dance, which was inspired by regimental
     concert parties with their tradition of poking fun at those in authority.
11   General Sir William Thwaites (1868–1947) Director of Military
     Intelligence from 1918 to 1922 and Director of Military Operations and
     Intelligence from 1922 to 1923.
12   Vernon Kell kept a list of former MI5 staff during the First World War
     for use in emergencies. In order to keep in touch with former staff, he
     founded the IP (Intelligence and Police) Dining Club, which met regularly
     up to the Second World War.
13   MI5 had 844 staff in November 1918, reduced to 151 by May 1920.
14   David Lloyd George (1863–1945), 1st Earl Lloyd-George of Dwyfor,
     Liberal politician and coalition government Prime Minister from
     1916 to 1922.

23 Steps Back to Normal

1   Baron Rodolphe d'Erlanger (1872–1932), French painter and
    musicologist specialising in the history of Arab music.
2   Anna Pavlova (1881–1931), prima ballerina of the Imperial Russian
    Ballet. Most famous for creating the role of the Dying Swan in 1905, a
    solo choreographed for her by Michel Fokine.
3   Emperor Hirohito of Japan (1901–1989), reigned from 1928 to 1989,
    undertook a six-month tour of Europe in 1921.
4   Major-General Sir Francis Piggott (1883–1966).
5   Michael Collins (1890–1922), Irish revolutionary leader, soldier and
    politician.
6   Kevin O'Higgins (1892–1927), Irish politician and Vice-President of the
    Executive Council from 1922 to 1927.
7   Colonel Sir Charles Wyndham Murray (1844–1929), Conservative MP
    from 1892 to 1906 and Chairman of the Japan Society from 1913 to 1918.
8   Florence van Raalte (née Clow) (1862–1952), owner of Brownsea Island
    and an acclaimed painter.
9   Ludovic Hurwitz Y Zender was shot on 11 April 1916. Telegrams
    from Zender to his handler in Norway attracted the attention of code

experts. Zender's telegrams purported to be orders for different kinds of tinned fish goods, but the wording varied suspiciously and in a way that resembled the code based upon orders for cigars that had been used by Janssen and Roos (see chapter 20, note 7).

10   General Sir John Burnett-Stuart (1875–1958), Director of Military Operations and Intelligence 1923–1926.

11   Dr Edvard Benes (1884–1948), President of Czechoslovakia 1935–1938 and 1945–1948, and President-in-exile 1939–1945.

12   Stanley Baldwin (1867–1947), 1st Earl Baldwin of Bewdley, Conservative Prime Minister 1923–January 1924, November 1924–1929 and 1935–1937.

13   James Ramsay MacDonald (1866–1937), first Labour Prime Minister from January to November 1924, 1929–1931, and Prime Minister of a national coalition government 1931–1935.

24 Visit to South Africa

1   During the 1926 general strike the War Office department MI(B), that collected and co-ordinated intelligence during the strike, comprised mostly retired MI5 officers under Kell's deputy Brigadier-General Sir Eric Holt-Wilson.

2   Vice-Admiral Sir Maurice Fitzmaurice (1870–1927), Director of Naval Intelligence 1921–1924 and Commander-in-Chief Africa Station 1924–1927. An accomplished organist, Fitzmaurice was a Director of the Royal Academy of Music and a member of the Royal College of Organists.

3   Field Marshal Jan Smuts (1870–1950), Prime Minister of South Africa 1919–1924 and 1939–1948. Led a Boer commando against the British in the Second Boer War. Following the creation of the Union of South Africa in 1909, Smuts formed the Union Defence Force in 1914. During the First World War he led South African forces against Germany, capturing German South-West Africa.

4   Colonel George de Stacpoole (1886–1965), 5th Duc de Stacpoole.

5   Norman Baillie-Stewart (1909–1962), a subaltern in the Seaforth Highlanders. Court-martialled in 1933 for selling military secrets to Germany, for which he received five years' imprisonment. Following

his release, Baillie-Stewart settled in Germany and became a German citizen in 1940. During the Second World War he was a propaganda broadcaster for the German propaganda ministry, receiving another five years' imprisonment for committing an act likely to assist the enemy.

6   John Graham Kell (1910–1979), second son of Sir Vernon and Lady Kell.

25 George VI Comes to the Throne

1   King Edward VIII (1894–1972), reigned from January 1936 until his abdication in December 1936.

2   On 16 July 1936 George Andrew McMahon, an Irish journalist and right-wing extremist thought to be mentally ill, raised a pistol at the King as his horse passed a crowd on Constitution Hill while returning to Buckingham Palace from a colours ceremony in Hyde Park. A woman in the crowd grabbed McMahon's arm and shouted, alerting a policeman who knocked the revolver from his hand.

3   Air Vice-Marshal Sir Philip Game (1876–1961), a senior RAF officer and Commissioner of the Metropolitan Police from 1935 to 1945.

4   General Sir Maurice Grove Taylor (1881–1960), 1934–1937 chief administration officer Aldershot command.

5   Sir Henry Walford Davies (1869–1941), British composer, conductor and educator. Musical adviser to the BBC, he became popular with radio audiences for his explanatory talks on music. Master of the King's Music 1934–1941.

6   General Sir William Bartholomew (1877–1962), Director of Military Operations and Intelligence 1931–1934.

7   Percy Glading was a Communist Party of Great Britain (CPGB) official, who ran a Soviet spy-ring inside Woolwich Arsenal, where he worked until he was dismissed in 1928. He was arrested in January 1938 and sentenced to six years' imprisonment. Albert Williams, who worked at Woolwich Arsenal, was a member of Glading's spy-ring. He received four years' imprisonment.

8   Joachim von Ribbentrop (1893–1946), Nazi ambassador to Britain 1936–1938 and Foreign Minister 1938–1945.

9   Robert Anthony Eden (1897–1977), 1ˢᵗ Earl of Avon, Foreign Secretary
     1935–1938, 1940–1945 and 1951–1955 and Conservative Prime
     Minister 1955–1957.

10   Sir Robert Russell Scott (1877–1960), Permanent Under-Secretary at the
     Home Office 1932–1938.

26 Preparation for a Second World War

1   In July 1939 MI5 had 36 officers (not including security control personnel
     at the ports); this increased to 102 in January 1940; and 230 in January
     1941. MI5 also had 133 secretarial and Registry staff in July 1939; this
     grew to 334 in January 1940; and 617 in January 1941.

2   George Steer (1909–1944), journalist, author and war correspondent
     who reported on the Second Italo-Abyssinian War and the Spanish Civil
     War. Joined the British Army in 1940 and led a forward propaganda unit
     in Abyssinia and Burma.

3   Emperor Haile Selassie I (1892–1975), ruler of Abyssinia/Ethiopia
     1930–1974.

4   Chiang Kai-shek (1877–1975), leader of the nationalist government of
     the Republic of China from 1927 to 1949 and President of Taiwan from
     1950 to 1975.

5   During the second quarter of 1940 MI5 received an average of 8,200
     requests for the vetting of individuals and the issue of exit permits per week.

6   Between September and November 1940, 25 German agents who landed
     in Britain by parachute or small boat were captured. Four of them were
     turned into double agents.

7   For most of the First World War, the government's policy had been to
     intern all enemy aliens unless they could prove that they posed no threat.
     MI5 favoured the same policy at the start of the Second World War.
     However the government decided that, rather than mass internment,
     tribunals would be established to individually review the cases of all male
     enemy aliens over 16 years of age. MI5 was given the impossible task
     of gathering concrete evidence in all of these cases. In December 1939
     80 per cent of MI5's time was spent on dealing with the alien population,
     leaving it with inadequate resources to investigate the threat from

German espionage. After the fall of France the government adopted a policy of mass internment.

8   Robert Vansittart (1881–1957), 1st Baron Vansittart, British diplomat and Permanent Under-Secretary at the Foreign Office 1930–1938. Known for his opposition to appeasement and strong stance against Nazi Germany. Also a published poet, novelist and playwright.

9   Isabel Jeans (1891–1985), British stage and film actress. Best known for her roles in several Alfred Hitchcock films and for her portrayal of aunt Alicia in the 1958 musical film 'Gigi'. She was married to barrister and playwright Gilbert Wakefield.

10 David Ivor Davies (1893–1951), better known as Ivor Novello, was a British composer and actor. He first achieved success as a songwriter, his first big hit 'Keep the Home Fires Burning' was hugely popular during the First World War. He turned to stage and film acting in the 1920s, starring in two silent Hitchcock films in 1927: 'The Lodger' and 'Downhill'.

11 Probably referring to Mathilde Krafft, a British citizen of German birth, who forwarded money for the German secret service. Krafft was identified by double agent SNOW but not arrested immediately for fear of compromising SNOW and in the hope that she might provide leads to other agents.

12 General Sir Geoffrey Scoones (1893–1975), commanded IV Corps of Lieutenant Slim's Fourteenth Army (see note below).

13 Field Marshal William Slim (1891–1970), 1st Viscount Slim, commanded the Fourteenth Army in the Burma campaign.

14 Dr Suzan Simpson (née Kell).

27 Resignation from MI5

1   Vere Ponsonby (1880–1956), 9th Earl of Bessborough, an MP from 1910 until 1920 when he was elevated to the House of Lords, and Governor-General of Canada from 1931 to 1935.

2   The Free French was the French government-in-exile during the Second World War, led by Charles de Gaulle. Free French military forces continued to fight against the Axis Powers as one of the Allies after the fall of France.

3   Colonel TRP Warren, Chief Constable of Buckinghamshire
     Constabulary 1928–1953.

4   George Johnson Armstrong (1902–1941), a marine engineer, was
     convicted of communicating with the German Consul in Boston, USA in
     order to offer him assistance before the USA entered the war, and hanged
     on 10 July 1941.

5   The Treachery Act 1940 was passed by Parliament in May 1940 to
     facilitate the prosecution and execution of enemy spies and saboteurs. It
     was considered necessary because treason still had its own special rules of
     evidence and procedure, set out in the Treason Act 1695, which made it
     a difficult offence to prove and prosecute. The new offence of treachery,
     a felony, was designed to make securing convictions easier as treachery
     could be proved under the same rules of evidence as ordinary offences.
     It was also necessary because there was doubt whether the treason laws
     were applicable to saboteurs.

6   Field Marshal Bernard Law Montgomery (1887–1976), 1st Viscount
     Montgomery of Alamein, commanded the British Eighth Army in the
     Western Desert during the Second World War.